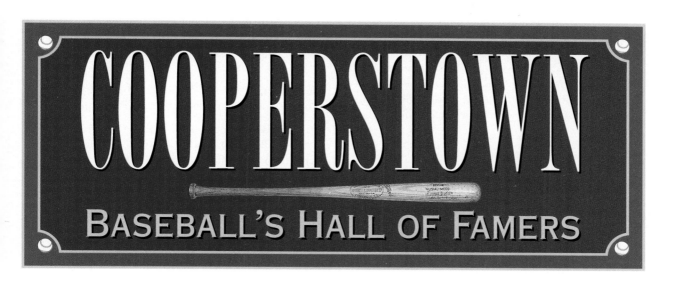

COOPERSTOWN
BASEBALL'S HALL OF FAMERS

Contributing writer and editor:
Paul Adomites

Contributing writers:
David Nemec
Matthew D. Greenberger
Dan Schlossberg
Dick Johnson
Mike Tully
Pete Palmer

PUBLICATIONS INTERNATIONAL, LTD.

Paul Adomites is the author of *October's Game*, is co-author of *Babe Ruth: His Life and Times* and *Best of Baseball*, and was a contributing writer for *Treasury of Baseball*, *Total Baseball*, and *Encyclopedia of Baseball Team Histories*. He served as publications director for the Society of American Baseball Research (SABR) and founded and edited *SABR Review of Books*, as well as its successor, the *Cooperstown Review*. He is a frequent contributor to *Pirates Magazine* and *In Pittsburgh*.

David Nemec is a baseball historian who has authored and co-authored numerous baseball history, quiz, and memorabilia books, including *Beer & Whisky League*, *Great Baseball Feats, Facts & Firsts*, *The Ultimate Baseball Book*, and *20th Century Baseball Chronicle*. He has consulted on such books as *Greatest Baseball Players of All Time* and *Baseball: More Than 150 Years*.

Matthew D. Greenberger is a freelance sportswriter and has been a contributing editor for *The Scouting Report* series, the commissioner for the Bill James Fantasy Baseball game, and a senior sports statistician for STATS, Inc. He was a contributing writer for *1991 Baseball Almanac* and has worked on the *Major League Handbook* series.

Dan Schlossberg is baseball editor for *American Encyclopedia Annual*, columnist for *Legends Magazine*, and contributor to *Petersen's Pro Baseball Yearbook*, *Street and Smith's Official Baseball Yearbook*, and many other baseball periodicals. The former Associated Press sportswriter has written 15 books, including *The Baseball Catalog* and *The Baseball Book of Why*.

Dick Johnson serves as curator of the Sports Museum of New England in Cambridge, Massachusetts, where he has mounted exhibits celebrating the achievements of the Boston Braves, Women in Sports, and the Boston Bruins. He is book review editor of *New England Sports Magazine* and is co-author of *Ted Williams: A Portrait in Words and Pictures* and *Young at Heart, The Story of Johnny Kelly*.

Mike Tully is a former national baseball writer for United Press International. He has written six books, including *Leagues and Barons* and *1990-91 Baseball's Hottest Rookies*. His freelance work has appeared in *The National Sports Daily*, *Sports Illustrated*, and *The New York Times*. He was a contributing writer for *1997 Baseball Almanac*.

Pete Palmer edited both *Total Baseball* and *The Hidden Game of Baseball* with John Thorn. Palmer was the statistician for *1997 Baseball Almanac*, *1996-97 Basketball Almanac*, and *1001 Fascinating Baseball Facts*. He is a member of the Society for American Baseball Research.

CONTENTS

Baseball's Hall of Famers

Cy Young

Cap Anson

Lefty Grove

Lou Gehrig

Joe DiMaggio

Chapter Five
EQUAL OPPORTUNITY

Jackie Robinson

Chapter Six
MANIFEST DESTINY

Chapter Seven
NEW FRONTIER

APPENDIX

INTRODUCTION

Enshrinement is the Highest Honor

The National Baseball Hall of Fame and Museum is the oldest and most revered of all the sports Halls of Fame. Enshrinement is the highest honor a major-league player can receive. The term "Hall of Fame" embraces all three branches of the sport's shrine: the gallery where the plaques of the Hall of Fame players hang, the adjacent museum, and the library.

Odds against election to the Hall are overwhelming: about 1,500-to-1 for the typical major-leaguer. To qualify for the ballot, a player must have played at least 10 years in the major leagues and be retired for five—requirements that are sometimes waived for special cases, such as the untimely death of Roberto Clemente in 1972.

A six-member screening committee prepares the annual ballot, and selected players remain eligible for 15 years—unless they receive less than five percent of the vote. That system keeps the ballot from becoming unwieldy. Electors must have covered major-league baseball for at least 10 years.

Various special committees have also been given the power to enshrine baseball personalities. They were the Centennial Commission of 1937 and '38, Old Timers Committee of 1939 to 1949, Negro Leagues Committee of 1971 to 1977, and current Veterans Committee, created in 1953. The Veterans Committee considers players retired at least 23 years who received at least 100 votes from the Baseball Writers' Association of America, and can enshrine managers, umpires, or executives but is permitted to name only one non-player per year.

Collecting 3,000 hits or winning 300 games does not produce an automatic ticket to Cooperstown. In fact, there is no statistical guideline. Voters are instructed to judge each candidate on ability, integrity, sportsmanship, character, and contribution to his teams and to baseball in general.

Early in the 20th century, a group of Cooperstown, New York, residents bought a lot that had been identified as the birthplace of baseball. In 1923, National League president John A. Heydler came to Cooperstown for the dedication of Doubleday Field. It was not until 1934, however, that a tattered, old baseball was discovered in a farmhouse attic in Fly Creek, a village three miles from Cooperstown. Since the trunk had belonged to Abner Graves, local historians leapt to the conclusion that the ball had been used by Abner Doubleday in the first baseball game.

Stephen C. Clark, a local resident, bought the ball for $5, enclosed it in a glass case, and placed it on the fireplace mantle of the Village Club, a combination library and boys club. After the addition of other baseball memorabilia, the exhibit became so popular that sentiment for a national museum soared. Clark took the idea to new National League president Ford Frick, who not only embraced

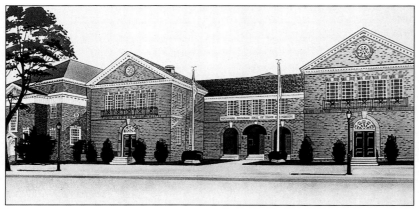

The Hall of Fame in Cooperstown, New York.

the concept but suggested the inclusion of a Hall of Fame for the game's heroes.

The Depression-weary baseball establishment—desperate for a gimmick that might start the turnstiles spinning again—began making elaborate plans for the game's 100th birthday. Those plans, announced in March 1936, would tie the Centennial with the museum, Hall of Fame, and Doubleday Field in a nationwide party. The village gym was converted into the National Baseball Hall of Fame and Museum.

To fill the Hall, there were two elections in 1936: one by 226 members of the Baseball Writers' Association of America and another by a special 78-member veterans committee. The only five players able to muster the required 75 percent of the vote were: Ty Cobb (222), Babe Ruth and Honus Wagner (215

Several of the all-time greats, such as Ty Cobb and Cy Young, receive their own display case inside the Hall.

each), Christy Mathewson (205), and Walter Johnson (189). The first election, plus three subsequent tallies, gave the Hall 26 members by the time it opened on June 12, 1939. All 11 living members appeared for the induction ceremonies.

Some of the treasures the shrine holds include the shoes of Shoeless Joe Jackson, Christy Mathewson's piano (with baseball bats as supporting legs), Babe Ruth's bowling ball, and a 17-foot bat carved as a gift for Ted Williams. The library's archives include hundreds of thousands of newspaper documents, photographs, videotapes, radio tapes, movie reels, sheet music, team files, team publications, baseball magazines, and documents of the game dating back to 1840.

The collection honors not only the relative handful of Hall of Fame players but also the game itself. It traces the game's history from pre-Civil War sandlot days through the development of domed ballparks, divisional play, and free agency. Although much of 19th-century baseball was played under rules and conditions that seem completely foreign to followers of today's game, Cooperstown remembers its heritage.

When Stan Musial retired, he owned every Cardinals career batting record except for highest batting average.

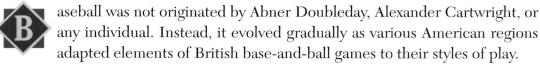
Baseball was not originated by Abner Doubleday, Alexander Cartwright, or any individual. Instead, it evolved gradually as various American regions adapted elements of British base-and-ball games to their styles of play.

The New York and Massachusetts games competed with many other versions for popularity. The New York version of "Base Ball" took precedence; the first organized team, Cartwright's Knickerbocker Base Ball Club, formed in 1845 and played the first game under his rules a year later. The Civil War put development of the game on hold but spread its popularity. An 1857 convention in New York City attended by 16 clubs formulated a single set of rules. The National Association of Base Ball Players, created by the convention, soon had over 200 members and countless fans.

Baseball's Wright Brothers—Harry and George—became the highest-paid members of the first all-professional team, the Cincinnati Red Stockings, in 1869. This team's prosperity emboldened professionals to form the National Association in 1871, making it the first modern professional league. Riddled by disorganization and financial hardship, the NA collapsed after five years. William Hulbert formed the National League in the NA's place in 1876.

The NL was a success, and it survives to this day, despite challenges from several rival leagues, including the American Association and the Players' League. By the turn of the century, however, the National League faced its most successful challenger.

This plate, from 1887, features four Hall of Famers: (clockwise from upper left) Mickey Welch, Monte Ward, Roger Connor, and Tim Keefe.

ALEXANDER JOY CARTWRIGHT

Baseball wasn't created; it evolved gradually from several different games. So we cannot credit the invention of baseball to any one individual. However, Alexander Cartwright—Alick, to his friends—had a large hand in the development of the game as it's now known.

Cartwright helped form the Knickerbocker Base Ball Club on September 23, 1845, and drafted a set of 20 rules that set baseball apart from other bat-and-ball games. The following spring, on June 19 at Elysian Field in Hoboken, New Jersey, the Knickerbockers played the first game under the new rules. With Cartwright umpiring, the Knickerbockers were drubbed by the New York Nine, 23-1.

Cartwright remained in New York until March 1, 1849, and then, lured by the Gold Rush, went to the West Coast. After a short, disillusioning time there, he set sail for Hawaii, where he lived until his death in 1892. Inducted in 1938.

HARRY WRIGHT

Harry Wright was selected for the Hall of Fame largely for his contributions as a baseball pioneer and innovator. British-born William Henry Wright was the son of a professional cricket player. After his family emigrated to New York, Wright joined the amateur Knickerbockers club as an outfielder.

Hired to organize the Cincinnati Red Stockings Base Ball team, Wright recruited the finest baseball players in the country, beginning with his brother George. His team won an amazing 130 consecutive games in 1869 and 1870 before losing a hair-raising extra-inning contest to the Brooklyn Atlantics. Wright moved to manage Boston in the National Association, the first

professional league, in 1871. His teams won every pennant but one during the loop's five-year existence.

Harry Wright managed for 18 more seasons in the National League, fathering such ideas as pregame batting practice and fungoing fly balls to outfielders before a game. Inducted in 1953.

MAJOR LEAGUE TOTALS			
BA	H	HR	RBI
.272	222	4	111

GEORGE WRIGHT

The star shortstop of the legendary Cincinnati Red Stockings team that went undefeated for the entire 1869 season, George Wright was elected to the Hall of Fame for his contributions as both a player and a baseball pioneer. When his brother Harry, a lesser athlete but a more influential trailblazer, joined him in Cooperstown 16 years later, the Wrights became the first pair of sib-

lings so enshrined. Inducted in 1937.

MAJOR LEAGUE TOTALS			
BA	H	HR	RBI
.302	867	11	330

HENRY CHADWICK

The only sportswriter honored in the Hall, British-born Henry Chadwick was called by Teddy Roosevelt the "Father of Baseball."

Chadwick designed a system for scoring a baseball contest remarkably like the modern box score. He was the first to compile reference books on baseball and instructional guides on how to play the game. Inducted in 1938.

AL SPALDING

By age 16, Albert Goodwill Spalding was already pitching for the Rockford Forest Citys, one of the top teams in the Midwest. Later he became the game's first magnate, not only owning teams but also creating a highly successful sporting goods franchise that still bears his name. Spalding was elected to the Hall of Fame as both a player and a baseball pioneer. Inducted in 1939.

MAJOR LEAGUE TOTALS			
W	L	ERA	K
252	65	2.04	227

CANDY CUMMINGS

William Arthur Cummings possessed a baffling curveball. Some historians believe he invented the pitch; others think that, at most, he played a part in its evolution. Cummings was inducted into the Hall of Fame with the first batch of immortals. Since his major-league career was so brief—he played just six seasons—his reputation as curveball creator must have inspired his election as a pioneer. Inducted in 1939.

MAJOR LEAGUE TOTALS			
W	L	ERA	K
145	94	2.39	257

MORGAN BULKELEY

Morgan Gardner Bulkeley is the most obscure person in the Hall of Fame. Because of his business credentials, he was chosen the first president of the National League in 1876 by its founder, William Hulbert. Bulkeley served for one year, then left baseball. In 1937, when it was agreed that Ban Johnson, the first president of the American League, should be among the original Hall enshrinees, it seemed appropriate that the first NL president should be likewise commemorated. Inducted in 1937.

CAP ANSON

Adrian Constantine "Cap" Anson's first five years in pro baseball were the five years of the National Association, the first professional league. When the National League was formed in 1876, he cast his lot with the Chicago White Stockings. He remained a fixture there for the next 22 seasons, setting a 19th-century loyalty record for the longest stint by a player with one team.

Initially a third baseman, Anson moved to first base when he became the club's manager in 1879. Never a strong fielder, he excelled as a batsman. Only three times in his 27-year career did he hit below .300, and he was the first player to accumulate 3,000 hits. Cap led the NL in RBI eight times from 1880 to 1891. Furthermore, he topped the loop three times in batting average and four times in slugging average. Anson led Chicago to five pennants.

Anson was no saint, however. His vile language on the field often led to fines, and rival fans called him "Crybaby" Anson because of his whining when events did not go his way. The racist Anson threatened to organize a strike before the 1885 season, effectively barring several black performers from the major leagues, a ban that lingered, albeit unofficially, until 1947.

After the 1897 campaign, White Stockings president James Hart demanded Anson's resignation. When Anson refused, he was fired. The White Stockings, minus Anson for the first time in their 23-year history, became known as the Orphans. Inducted in 1939.

MAJOR LEAGUE TOTALS			
BA	H	HR	RBI
.333	3,418	97	2,076

WILLIAM HULBERT

William A. Hulbert was the man who gave baseball the business structure it has today. It was his idea to have baseball run by businessmen owners rather than players. In 1876, Hulbert helped create the National League. As NL leader, he dealt with some of baseball's early problems such as gambling, excessive drinking, and loose organization. He also took steps toward building the game's first dynasty, the Chicago White Stockings. Inducted in 1995.

KING KELLY

With a career shortened by alcoholism and because of a general disinclination to take care of himself, King Kelly is viewed by many historians as a colorful but vastly overrated performer whose press clippings far exceeded his deeds on the diamond. The truth is, for at least a few years, he may have been the best player in the game, batting as high as .388 while playing all over the diamond. And Kelly was the first true celebrity player in the style of Babe Ruth. Inducted in 1945.

MAJOR LEAGUE TOTALS			
BA	H	HR	RBI
.308	1,813	69	950

JIM O'ROURKE

James Henry O'Rourke was called "Orator" because he was the most eloquent player of the 19th century. O'Rourke was the first player in major-league history active in four different decades. Oddly, although he played every position on the diamond during his career, he never excelled at any of them. Somewhat of a liability in the field, the Orator made up for it by being a reliable and productive hitter. Inducted in 1945.

MAJOR LEAGUE TOTALS			
BA	H	HR	RBI
.311	2,643	62	1,203

PUD GALVIN

One of the most colorful performers in the last century, James Francis "Pud" Galvin is the only pitcher in history to win 20 or more games on 10 different occasions without ever

playing on a pennant-winning team. Owing partly to this piece of bad luck and partly to never being a league leader in any of the three triple-crown pitching departments—wins, strikeouts, or ERA—Galvin was not elected to the Hall of Fame until 1965 despite collecting 364 career victories, more than any other hurler who played exclusively in the 19th century.

"Pud" reportedly got his odd nickname because he made a hitter look like a pudding, a 19th-century slang term for a dud. In addition, he was called "Gentle Jeems" because he was a mild, unassuming individual who rarely drank or questioned umpires. Inducted in 1965.

MAJOR LEAGUE TOTALS			
W	L	ERA	K
364	310	2.85	1,807

MONTE WARD

John Montgomery Ward compiled 108 major-league wins before his 21st birthday. On the morning of June 17, 1880, Ward tossed a per-

fect 5-0 victory over Buffalo, missing by only five days the distinction of becoming the first pitcher to hurl a full nine-inning game without allowing a single baserunner. When his arm went sour, he became one of the better-fielding shortstops of his time and a more-than-competent offensive performer, good enough to collect 2,105 hits and twice pace the National League in stolen bases. Besides his playing credentials, Ward organized the Brotherhood of Professional Base Ball Players (an early attempt at player unionization) and was later a manager, owner, and chair of the rules committee. Few, if any, players or executives in the last century made a greater contribution to the game than Ward. Inducted in 1964.

MAJOR LEAGUE TOTALS			
W	L	ERA	K
164	102	2.10	920

OLD HOSS RADBOURN

Charley Gardner Radbourn gave himself the nickname Old Hoss. During the extraordinary 1884 season, in the midst of winning a record 59 games for the Providence Grays, Radbourn would warm up in the outfield until he finally proclaimed, "Old Hoss is ready." By the end of the season, Old Hoss had logged so many innings he could scarcely lift his arm to comb his hair.

There is no disputing that Radbourn was the game's supreme pitcher—for one year anyway. Recalled from a suspension for drunkenness in 1884 when his team's only other pitcher jumped leagues, he hurled nearly every game. His team won the flag by 10½ games. After winning 165 games in his first four years in the National League, Radbourn collected just 144 more victories before his wing finally gave out altogether during the 1891 campaign. Inducted in 1939.

MAJOR LEAGUE TOTALS			
W	L	ERA	K
309	195	2.67	1,830

DAN BROUTHERS

By any standard, Dennis Joseph "Dan" Brouthers was the greatest hitter in the game's first era (1871-1893, when the distance to the pitcher's mound was set at its present distance of 60'6"). Brouthers captured five hitting titles and, at

one time or another, led the league in every major batting department. In 1881, Big Dan teamed with Deacon White, Hardy Richardson, and Jack Rowe to give the Buffalo Bisons an attack so devastating the quartet was labeled "The Big Four." Brouthers topped the circuit in batting in 1882 and 1883.

The franchise was sold to Detroit, where Brouthers led the league in homers in 1886. The following season, he sparked the Wolverines to their only pennant. In 1890 he won a flag with the Boston Reds in the Players' League, and the following season he was on the pennant-winning Boston Reds in the American Association. He played on one last pennant winner in 1894 with the fabled Baltimore Orioles. Inducted in 1945.

MAJOR LEAGUE TOTALS			
BA	H	HR	RBI
.342	2,296	106	1,296

TIM KEEFE

As did virtually all the 19th century's 300-game winners, Timothy John Keefe had the luxury of playing for good teams for the better part of his career. In an era when most quality pitchers started upward of 50 games a season, winning 30 or 35 games with a contender was a routine matter, provided a hurler was durable—and Keefe was certainly that. In his first nine full seasons in the major leagues, he labored 4,087 innings

and racked up 285 victories. He totaled 342 wins, the eighth most in history. Keefe supplemented his fastball with a wicked curve, and some say he threw the first change-up. With Mickey Welch, he helped carry the Giants to National League pennants in 1888 and 1889. After his pitching career ended, he was an umpire for two years but could not stand the abuse and quit. Inducted in 1964.

MAJOR LEAGUE TOTALS			
W	L	ERA	K
342	225	2.62	2,560

MICKEY WELCH

Michael Francis Welch's major-league career was the second shortest of any 300-game winner. Only Old Hoss Radbourn toiled fewer than Welch's 13 seasons. As a rookie for the Troy Trojans of the National League in 1880, Welch notched 34 wins in 64 starts and 574 innings. Teaming up with Tim Keefe on two different teams, Welch topped the 30-win mark three more times on his way to 307 career wins. Inducted in 1973.

Major League Totals			
W	L	ERA	K
307	210	2.71	1,850

ROGER CONNOR

Roger Connor was one of the game's first noteworthy sluggers. The beefy Connor's 233 career triples are fifth on the all-time list and first among players active solely in the last century. He was also the only pre-1900 player to collect more than 1,000 walks. His 138 home runs stood as the career record until Babe Ruth surpassed the mark. Inducted in 1976.

Major League Totals			
BA	H	HR	RBI
.317	2,467	138	1,322

BUCK EWING

In 1919, Francis Richter, one of the leading sportswriters of the day, deemed Buck Ewing, Ty Cobb, and Honus Wagner the three greatest players in baseball to that time. Richter went on to say that Ewing might have been the best of them all according to "supreme excellence in all departments—batting, catching, fielding, baserunning, throwing, and baseball brains—a player without a weakness of any kind, physical, mental, or tempera-

mental." From the very outset of his career, Ewing was viewed as an outstanding defensive catcher, the most demanding position—even more demanding then than now.

Ewing was one of the first catchers to catalogue each opposing batter's weakness then share the knowledge in pregame clubhouse meetings. John Foster wrote that "as a thrower to bases, Ewing never had a superior. Ewing was the man of whom it was said, 'he handed the ball to the second baseman from the batter's box.'" Catchers in the last century seldom worked more than half their team's games. While most backstops simply took that day off, Ewing customarily played another position. So versatile was Buck that he could fill in anywhere on the diamond. In 1936, he tied for first place in the initial vote of the old-timers for the Hall of Fame. Inducted in 1936.

Major League Totals			
BA	H	HR	RBI
.303	1,625	71	883

TOMMY McCARTHY

Thomas Francis Michael McCarthy was named to the Hall of Fame in 1946, long before other players who produced career statistical totals nearly double his. McCarthy's claim to fame was that he and Hugh Duffy were the Boston Beaneaters' famous "Heavenly Twins" of the early 1890s. The Irish duo swiftly became the darlings of Boston fans. Duffy was by far the better player, but McCarthy had his moments as well. In 1890, he batted .350 with 83 stolen bases. Inducted in 1946.

Major League Totals			
BA	H	HR	RBI
.292	1,496	44	735

JOHN CLARKSON

In almost every respect, John Gibson Clarkson, the son of a wealthy jewelry manufacturer, was badly out of place in the rough-and-tumble era in which he played. The miracle is not so much that he won 328 games but that he played 12 seasons in the majors before his sensitive nature overcame him. Clarkson's 53 wins in 1885, (at age 23), is the second-highest victory total ever. Inducted in 1963.

Major League Totals			
W	L	ERA	K
328	178	2.81	1,978

BILLY HAMILTON

Inordinately small as a boy, chunky, and equipped with heavy legs, William Robert Hamilton seemed to have little future in baseball. If he had any chance at all, it would seem to have been as a catcher. As it turned out, Hamilton became the speediest center fielder and most prolific base thief of his time. Moreover, he scored 1,690 runs in 1,591 games to become one of only two players in major-league history to average more than a run per game. (Harry Stovey of the old American Association is the other.)

Hamilton stole more than 96 bases five times and three times surpassed 100 steals. He led his league in walks and on-base percentage five times each, and his lifetime batting average of .344 is second only to Ed Delahanty among 19th-century stars. Inducted in 1961.

MAJOR LEAGUE TOTALS			
BA	H	HR	RBI
.344	2,158	40	736

SAM THOMPSON

Samuel Luther Thompson was already 25 years old when he broke into the majors with the Detroit Wolverines in early July 1885. Claiming the right field job, he led Detroit in batting in 1886, and led the entire National League in 1887, hitting .372 and bagging a 19th-century-record 166 RBI. Still, Thompson's talents as a hitter went largely unrecognized (RBI totals were kept only informally). It was not until long after Thompson retired that historians revealed him to be the most prolific RBI man ever—.921 per game. The home run, another Thompson specialty, was regarded as trivial by many "experts" of that era.

Thompson, however, was not merely a slugger. He also led the National League on three occasions in hits, twice in doubles, and once in triples. A good outfielder, he had one of the strongest arms in the game. Inducted in 1974.

MAJOR LEAGUE TOTALS			
BA	H	HR	RBI
.331	1,979	127	1,299

HUGH DUFFY

For years, Hugh Duffy was listed in the record books as the player with the highest single-season batting average in major-league history (.438 in 1894). A recent reexamination of that season's box scores revealed that the record books have been wrong all this time: Duffy actually hit .440 that year.

On the other hand, a similar reassessment altered Duffy's career batting average from .330 to .324, and most of his other career totals have also suffered a reduction. Even after the modification of his achievements, however, Duffy remains one of the outstanding hitters of the last century. The 5'9" and slender Duffy (his first manager, Cap Anson, thought he was a batboy) later paired up with Tommy McCarthy on the Boston Beaneaters and became known as one of the "Heavenly Twins." Inducted in 1945.

MAJOR LEAGUE TOTALS			
BA	H	HR	RBI
.324	2,282	106	1,302

ED DELAHANTY

Some analysts consider Edward James Delahanty the greatest right-handed hitter of all time. The most famous and eldest member of the only family to send five brothers to the majors, he batted over .400 three times. Yet, with the sole exception of Lou Gehrig, Delahanty is baseball's most tragic figure.

Called "Big Ed" more for his strength than his size, Delahanty played for the Phillies all but one of his first 14 seasons. From 1891 through 1895, he led their potent hitting attack, strong enough to bat a team-record-setting .407 in 1894, but not strong enough to win a flag.

Delahanty longed to play on a pennant winner. He had a deal in early 1903 to join the New York Giants, but a peace settlement between the two leagues froze all players with their old teams. Stuck in Washington, owing manager John McGraw money and experiencing marital trouble, Delahanty grew despondent and began drinking heavily. On the night of July 2, 1903, he was ejected from a train that was about to cross the International Bridge over Niagara Falls. Drunk and frustrated, he set off in pursuit of the locomotive but had difficulty negotiating the railway ties. He tumbled through the ties and plunged to his death into the river. Inducted in 1945.

MAJOR LEAGUE TOTALS			
BA	H	HR	RBI
.346	2,596	101	1,464

AMOS RUSIE

Amos Wilson Rusie is one of the few players in the Hall of Fame to spend fewer than 10 full seasons in the major leagues, his career abbreviated by two bitter holdouts.

In 1890, the 19-year-old Rusie led all National League hurlers with 341 strikeouts. As a New York Giant, he fell prey to the glitters of Gotham. By the time he was in his early 20s, he had a drinking problem. Worse, he could not escape the vindictive, cheap Andrew Freedman, one of the worst owners in the most repressive era in major-league history.

In the pitcher's box, however, "The Hoosier Thunderbolt" was in his element. More than any other hurler, Rusie prompted the last significant change in the geometric design of the playing field. During the 1892 season, batting averages plummeted to a record low. The game's rulemakers then decided to move the pitching distance to home plate from 50' to 60'6". Inducted in 1977.

MAJOR LEAGUE TOTALS			
W	L	ERA	K
246	174	3.07	1,950

JAKE BECKLEY

Jacob Peter Beckley, nicknamed "Eagle Eye," ended his professional baseball career with the record for playing the most games at first base (a record that has since been broken by Eddie Murray). But because Beckley left the game with 2,930 hits (just 70 short of the coveted 3,000 benchmark), and he died at age 50 in 1918, he didn't reach the Hall of Fame until 1971. Inducted in 1971.

MAJOR LEAGUE TOTALS			
BA	H	HR	RBI
.308	2,930	86	1,575

NED HANLON

As their manager, Edward Hugh Hanlon was the man who taught the legendary Baltimore Orioles of the 1890s their unique brand of ball—tough, no-holds-barred, "scientific" baseball. They were credited with innovating the hit-and-run, platooning, and especially skillful bunting: All tactics are still part of the game today. At one time, Hanlon had six future Hall of Famers on his Oriole team. Several, including John McGraw, became highly successful managers themselves later. Inducted in 1996.

MAJOR LEAGUE TOTALS		
W	L	PCT
1,313	1,164	.530

KID NICHOLS

When he joined the Boston Beaneaters in 1890, Charles Augustus Nichols looked so youthful and so physically unprepossessing he was called "Kid." Nichols is the only 300-game winner in major-league history who earned his success with just one pitch. He had a fastball, period. And it was by no means overpowering at that. What Nichols did possess in spades, however, was control. Nichols used a late-addition changeup sparingly. Until the end of his career, his fastball remained his "out" pitch.

Nichols won 27 games as a rookie in 1890 and 297 games in his first 10 seasons, more than any other pitcher during the 1890s. On seven occasions he collected 30 or more victories, reaching a high of 35 in 1892. Inducted in 1949.

MAJOR LEAGUE TOTALS			
W	L	ERA	K
361	208	2.95	1,873

JESSE BURKETT

In his first season as a regular with the Cleveland Spiders, Jesse Cail Burkett hit just .275. He nevertheless ranked among the club's top batters as averages all over the National League were down in 1892, the last season in which the pitchers' box was only 50′ from home plate. When 10′6″ were added to the span the next year,

Burkett's average jumped to .348; he didn't bat below .340 again until 1902. In the nine intervening seasons, Burkett twice topped the .400 mark and on three occasions led the National League in batting.

Popular with sportswriters because of his readiness to discuss hitting, Burkett was less of a hit with fans. His surly manner and frequent battles with umpires early in his career earned him the nickname "The Crab," but when the subject was batting, he was always an amiable host, even for kids. Inducted in 1946.

MAJOR LEAGUE TOTALS			
BA	H	HR	RBI
.338	2,850	75	952

HUGHIE JENNINGS

Hugh Ambrose Jennings was a team leader and shortstop for the legendary Baltimore Orioles of the 1890s, belting .401 in 1896. Manager Ned Hanlon named him captain, and his talents emerged when he became a manager himself. After several years learning his trade in the minors, Jennings took his Tigers to the World Series in each of his first three years at the helm, 1907-1909. Inducted in 1945.

MAJOR LEAGUE TOTALS			
BA	H	HR	RBI
.311	1,527	18	840

JOE KELLEY

Joseph James Kelley was a good outfielder and a productive hitter who learned his trade when Orioles manager Ned Hanlon made Joe his pet project. In 1893, Hanlon took Kelley out to the park early every morning to work on improving his fielding and hitting fundamentals. Kelley became the most complete player on the NL's best team during the mid-1890s. Inducted in 1971.

MAJOR LEAGUE TOTALS			
BA	H	HR	RBI
.317	2,220	65	1,194

CHARLES COMISKEY

Charles Albert Comiskey was a fine first baseman. As player-manager, he led the St. Louis Browns to American Association pennants from 1885 to 1888. Later, as owner of the Chicago White Sox, his cheap attitude toward his players overshadowed his accomplishments. Comiskey nourished, with his vision and industry, the creation of the American League. However, his greed nearly destroyed it, as his players conspired to throw the 1919 World Series in the infamous Black Sox Scandal. Inducted in 1939.

MAJOR LEAGUE TOTALS			
BA	H	HR	RBI
.264	1,530	29	883

Chapter Two
DEAD-BALL ERA

Emergence of the AL

he National League's decision to reduce to eight clubs in 1900 created a reservoir of surplus talent and unoccupied ballparks—and a climate conducive to the launch of a rival major league.

In the late 1890s, Ban Johnson had built the Western League into a minor-league power. In 1901, he renamed it the American League and declared it a major league. The AL filled former NL territories and planted rival clubs in both Philadelphia and Chicago. Using high salaries as bait, the upstart AL convinced many established stars to switch leagues. In January 1903, the NL came to terms with the AL, and the two leagues put together a new National Agreement. There were to be no changes in the baseball map for 50 years.

At the start of the 20th century, teams manufactured runs through bunts, hit-and-run plays, and stolen bases. Pitchers used trick deliveries and applied foreign substances to the ball. The balls themselves were so dead that swinging for the fences was futile. Pitchers were expected to work long and often; relief pitching was as rare as a home run.

At the end of 1920, eight members of the Chicago White Sox were accused of fixing the 1919 World Series against the Cincinnati Reds. The eight Black Sox were banned for life by Kenesaw Mountain Landis—baseball's first commissioner.

Christy Mathewson was baseball's original role model, and he was the game's best pitcher in the first decade of this century.

WILLIE KEELER

Nicknamed "Wee Willie" because of his 5′4″, 120-pound stature, William Henry Keeler, in spite of his size, compiled 2,932 hits and 1,719 runs, twice led the National League in batting, and posted a .341 career batting average. His forte, as he himself put it, was to "hit 'em where they ain't," and there has probably never been a batter more skillful at poking a ball through a hole in the infield or executing a hit-and-run play. Keeler was an integral member of one of baseball's most famous teams—the 1894-1898 Baltimore Orioles. While his teammates played the reckless, exciting, and at times deceitful brand of baseball for which the team became renowned, Keeler was shy and retiring almost to the point of invisibility. Were it not for his small size, he might, curiously, have gone without notice. But barely bigger than a batboy, Keeler became instead a fan favorite. Inducted in 1939.

MAJOR LEAGUE TOTALS			
BA	**H**	**HR**	**RBI**
.341	2,932	33	810

CY YOUNG

A Young-autographed baseball.

Shortly after signing with Canton of the Tri-State League in 1890, the 23-year-old Cy Young was spotted warming up throwing at a wooden fence. The damage to the barrier, legend has it, was like that of a cyclone hitting it. An enterprising sportswriter shortened "cyclone" to "Cy," and Young would never again be known by any other name during his professional career.

Denton True Young made his big-league debut with the Cleveland Spiders on August 6, 1890. Throughout the 1890s, Young, Kid Nichols, and Amos Rusie vied for recognition as top pitcher in the game. Although Nichols pitched for the best team and collected the most wins, and Rusie regularly logged the most strikeouts and lowest ERAs, it was Young who reached the top of the league in all three departments. He blended stamina, guile, and excellent control in almost equal measures to make him a pitcher who rarely had a bad game. A pennant for the Spiders never materialized, however, and Young and most of the team's other stars were shipped to St. Louis in 1899.

Turning 33 years old in 1900, Young slipped to just 19 wins, his lowest output since his rookie season. He deserted the club to sign with Boston in the new American League, led the yearling major league in wins in 1901, then repeated his feat the next two years.

Cy went on to win 20 or more games six times for the Boston Americans, pitch on two pennant winners, and participate in the first modern World Series in 1903. Perhaps the finest effort of his career came on May 5, 1904, when he pitched a perfect game to beat Rube Waddell of Philadelphia 3-0.

Sold to Cleveland at age 42 in 1909, Young again defied time by leading the Naps mound staff with 19 wins. It was his last good season. Two years later, Young retired with 511 career victories. To the day he last took off his uniform, he boasted that he had never had a sore arm or spent a single minute on the trainer's table.

Young felt wounded when he was passed over in the initial Hall of Fame election in 1936. The oversight was rectified the following year, however, making him among the original group of inductees. Shortly after his death on November 4, 1955, baseball instituted the Cy Young Award, an annual honor bestowed upon the most valuable pitcher in each league. Inducted in 1937.

MAJOR LEAGUE TOTALS			
W	L	ERA	K
511	316	2.63	2,803

VIC WILLIS

A big right-hander with a wicked curveball, Vic Willis gained a reputation for durability, winning at least 20 games eight times. In 1902, he set a major-league record with 45 complete games. In six of his eight seasons in Boston, the durable hurler threw more than 300 innings. Willis pitched for the Boston Beaneaters, Pittsburgh Pirates, and St. Louis Cardinals, fashioning a lifetime 249-205 record and a 2.63 ERA. Inducted in 1995.

MAJOR LEAGUE TOTALS			
W	L	ERA	K
249	205	2.63	1,651

FRED CLARKE

Fred Clarke is among the few members of the Hall of Fame who could justifiably have been selected as either a player or a manager. When he let go of the Pittsburgh reins at the conclusion of the 1915

season, he had racked up a then-record 1,602 managerial wins. Clarke concluded his career with a .312 batting average (a mark that would likely have been higher had he not been burdened with the dual job of playing and managing for much of his career). After acting as player-manager with Louisville, Clarke moved to the same job in Pittsburgh in the consolidation of the two teams. Beginning in 1901, he skippered the Pirates to three straight pennants, then won again in 1909 after narrowly missing the flag in 1908. Inducted in 1945.

MAJOR LEAGUE TOTALS			
BA	H	HR	RBI
.312	2,672	67	1,015

BOBBY WALLACE

When Rhoderick John "Bobby" Wallace was inducted into the Hall of Fame, he was the first American League shortstop enshrined. Since Wallace never played on a pennant winner, was a failure as a manager, and had a career batting average of only .268, the presumed reason for his selection is that he was a great fielder. By 1901, Wallace was generally recognized as the best shortstop in the majors. Inducted in 1953.

MAJOR LEAGUE TOTALS			
BA	H	HR	RBI
.268	2,309	34	1,121

JIMMY COLLINS

By 1908, the year that Home Run Baker debuted with the Philadelphia Athletics, major-league baseball had existed for 36 seasons. Yet only one third baseman who played before Baker is in the Hall of Fame. Simply put, Jimmy Collins was the most outstanding third sacker in the last century.

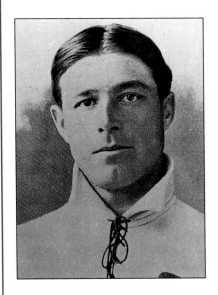

Those who witnessed James Joseph Collins play claimed he was without even a close rival. The first to charge bunts and play them barehanded, he also could range equally well toward the line or into the shortstop's territory to his left. Playing for the Boston Beaneaters in 1899, he accepted a record 629 chances. The following year, he set a 20th-century mark when he accumulated 252 putouts. Collins ended his career in Philadelphia; his replacement was Baker, the only time in history that one future Hall of Fame third baseman was succeeded by another. Inducted in 1945.

MAJOR LEAGUE TOTALS			
BA	H	HR	RBI
.294	1,999	65	983

NAP LAJOIE

In 1896, the Phillies purchased Napoleon Lajoie. Lajoie jumped to the Philadelphia Athletics of the fledgling American League in 1901 when A's manager Connie Mack offered him a four-year, $6,000-per-season pact. Lajoie responded with a 20th-century batting record of .426 and the Triple Crown.

A judge's ruling on Lajoie's actions sent him to Cleveland. With all the legal wrangling, Lajoie got into only 87 games in 1902, but he made up for the setback by winning the hitting titles in 1903 and 1904.

In all, Lajoie won four American League bat crowns. For the first 13 years of the 20th century, he was the American League's equivalent of Honus Wagner—the greatest fielder of his time at his position

who was also one of the greatest hitters.

Unlike Wagner, Lajoie was never on a championship team. The closest he came was in 1908, when Cleveland lost the pennant to Detroit by a half game. Lajoie was then in his fourth season as Cleveland's player-manager. He was so popular the team was renamed the "Naps" in his honor.

Although Lajoie stepped down as manager after 1909, he remained with Cleveland for five more seasons as a second baseman. Inducted in 1937.

MAJOR LEAGUE TOTALS			
BA	H	HR	RBI
.338	3,242	83	1,599

ROGER BRESNAHAN

If Hall of Fame membership was based on ongoing contributions and involvement in some of the most memorable incidents in baseball, then Roger Philip Bresnahan is among the Hall's most qualified members. He developed shin guards and a chest protector for catchers. Elected to the Hall of Fame one year after his death, Bresnahan became the first catcher honored in Cooperstown. Inducted in 1945.

MAJOR LEAGUE TOTALS			
BA	H	HR	RBI
.279	1,252	26	530

RUBE WADDELL

The baseball public knew George Edward Waddell only as Rube. Although Waddell detested the nickname, he was so uneducated and so ill-equipped to deal with even the simple exigencies of life that he seemed born to be called Rube. He was a man-child, physically powerful but childlike in his love of partying and chasing fire engines. Only Connie Mack was able to even come close to controlling him.

At the art of pitching a baseball, however, there have been few more worldly. In each of his first four seasons with the Athletics, Waddell was a 20-game winner and led the AL in strikeouts. His best overall campaign was 1904, when he collected 25 victories and fanned 349 hitters, a modern single-season record that endured until 1965.

Early in 1912, Waddell developed tuberculosis after working shoulder-deep in an icy flooding Kentucky river to help save a near-

(continued on page 22)

HONUS WAGNER

Growing up in an ethnic suburb of Pittsburgh, John Peter Wagner was more commonly known as Johannes or Hans, and the former was shortened to "Honus."

Wagner was a rarity, the son of an immigrant father who thought baseball was an acceptable profession. In his first two and a half seasons with the Louisville Colonels of the National League, Wagner hit .321. He was so versatile in the field that he never had a regular position. The Colonels used him at first base, second base, third base, and the outfield. When the franchise folded after the 1899 season, owner Barney Dreyfuss moved to Pittsburgh and took his best players with him.

Used mainly in the outfield in 1900, Wagner won the first of his

Wagner's 1910 American Tobacco Company baseball card sold for $451,000 in 1991.

still-record eight National League batting titles and also led the loop in doubles, triples, and slugging average. The 1902 Pirates won the pennant by a record 27½ games, and when Wagner was reluctantly installed at shortstop, they triumphed for a third successive season in 1903, and Wagner finally had a position he could call his own.

Even in his time Wagner was regarded as a folk hero. A model of clean living, he once had a baseball card of him removed from circulation because it was distributed in cigarette packs. The few copies of the card that survive are now each worth more than the total amount of salary Wagner made during his career. Ironically a later baseball

card of Wagner, made when he was a Pittsburgh coach, shows him preparing to ingest a wad of chewing tobacco.

Since Wagner's retirement as a player in 1917, his name has appeared in the shortstop slot on almost everyone's all-time All-Star Team. Some rate him the greatest player ever.

Wagner was so great a fielder that his contemporaries must have considered it cruel luck that he was also blessed with such incredible talent as a hitter and baserunner. During his 21-year career, Wagner was a league-leader at least twice in every major offensive department (including steals five times) except home runs and walks. When he retired, he had compiled more hits, runs, total bases, RBI, and stolen bases than any player in history. All these records have since been broken, but no other shortstop in the game's long history has even approached Wagner's overall achievements.

Wagner was among the elite group of five players named to the Hall of Fame when the first vote for enshrinement was conducted. Inducted in 1936.

MAJOR LEAGUE TOTALS			
BA	H	HR	RBI
.327	3,415	101	1,732

(continued from page 20)
by town. He died on April 1, 1914. Inducted in 1946.

MAJOR LEAGUE TOTALS			
W	L	ERA	K
193	143	2.16	2,316

ELMER FLICK

A great hitter, Elmer Harrison Flick was almost traded even-up for Ty Cobb. Flick produced several fine seasons: Three times he paced the AL in triples, once he led it in runs, and in 1905 he topped all AL hitters with a .308 average, the lowest figure to win a batting crown before 1968. Disabled by a mysterious stomach ailment and other nagging injuries, Flick never played regularly after the 1907 season. Inducted in 1963.

MAJOR LEAGUE TOTALS			
BA	H	HR	RBI
.313	1,752	48	756

TOM CONNOLLY

Thomas Henry Connolly was a rarity in his day: a great umpire who had never served a stint as a ballplayer. Born in England, Connolly came to America at age 15 and soon became fascinated by the rules of baseball. He had the honor of umpiring the first American League game on April 24, 1901, and in 1903 he was selected to

umpire in the first modern World Series between Boston and Pittsburgh. Inducted in 1953.

JACK CHESBRO

On October 10, 1904, the last day of the season, a wild pitch by John Dwight Chesbro cost the New York Highlanders a chance for the pennant. Had Chesbro won the game it would have been his 42nd victory. He had won more than 20 games three times for the Pirates and New Yorkers, and would top 20 once again, but his greatest defeat came during the season of his greatest triumphs. Inducted in 1946.

MAJOR LEAGUE TOTALS			
W	L	ERA	K
198	132	2.68	1,265

JOE MCGINNITY

Although he acquired his "Iron Man" nickname because he was an

ironworker, Joseph Jerome McGinnity could have earned the alias for his pitching exploits. In 1901, McGinnity became the first 20th-century pitcher to work both ends of a twin bill, accomplishing the feat twice with Baltimore of the American League. In mid-1902, McGinnity joined his former manager John McGraw in jumping to the NL Giants, where McGinnity remained for the rest of his 10-year major-league career, topping the NL in wins three times. In 1903, he won a record three doubleheaders in a single month and set a 20th-century National League record with 44 complete games. At his pinnacle in 1904, he bagged 35 victories and combined with Christy Mathewson for 68 wins, a 20th-century record for two pitchers on the same team. In his first eight big-league seasons, McGinnity averaged more than 37 starts per year and won 217 games. Inducted in 1946.

MAJOR LEAGUE TOTALS			
W	L	ERA	K
246	142	2.66	1,068

SAM CRAWFORD

In Sam Crawford's time, the mark of a great slugger was not home runs but triples. By that standard Samuel Earl Crawford was the dead-ball era's most prolific long-ball hitter. He retired in 1917 with 309 triples. Crawford still holds the distinction of being the only player

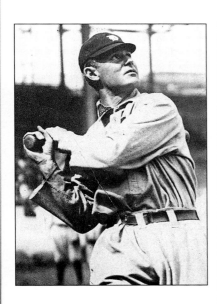

in this century to lead both major leagues in home runs.

After three-plus years with Cincinnati, Crawford seized his chance to escape the lowly Reds by jumping to Detroit in the American League in late 1902. Wahoo Sam promptly hit .335 in his first year with the Bengals and cracked 25 triples, an AL record that stood until 1912, when Joe Jackson notched 26 three-baggers. When Ty Cobb joined the Tigers in 1905, the team improved greatly. While not the high-average hitter that Cobb was, Crawford was his superior as an extra-base-hit producer. Playing side by side in the same outfield, the pair spearheaded the Tigers from 1907 to 1909, the years in which they became the first team in American League history to garner three consecutive pennants.

Crawford fashioned a .309 career batting average in 2,517 games and logged at least 10 triples in every full season he played. He was a loop leader in three-baggers

six times and also topped the AL on three occasions in RBI. Inducted in 1957.

MAJOR LEAGUE TOTALS			
BA	H	HR	RBI
.309	2,961	97	1,525

CHRISTY MATHEWSON

Christopher Mathewson probably did more than any other performer of his day to enhance the image of a professional baseball player. Educated, intelligent, and a consummate gentleman, he seemed almost too good to be true. And after 17 years in the majors, he had 373 victories and an almost universal recognition as the greatest pitcher in National League history to that time.

Originally Giant property, Mathewson was drafted away by Cincinnati, but a sneaky trade for the aged

Amos Rusie brought Matty back to New York. After winning 20 games for the Giants in 1901, Matty tumbled to just 14 victories the next year. However, he then reeled off 12 straight 20-win seasons, including four of 30-plus, with a high of 37 in 1908. The net result of his extraordinary run of success was that he had 300 career victories by the time he was 32 years old.

In 1905, in his first World Series appearance, Mathewson twirled a record three complete-game shutouts and 27 scoreless innings against the Philadelphia Athletics, a performance generally considered the most outstanding in World Series history.

In 1916, with his famed screwball or "fadeaway" no longer effective, Mathewson was traded to Cincinnati to manage. While serving overseas in World War I, he accidentally inhaled poison gas, permanently damaging his lungs. He died on October 7, 1925. Christy Mathewson was among the first group of five players elected to the Hall of Fame. Inducted in 1936.

MAJOR LEAGUE TOTALS			
W	L	ERA	K
373	188	2.13	2,502

EDDIE PLANK

Although nearly age 26 when he graduated from Gettysburg College in 1901, Edward Stewart Plank was signed by Connie Mack of the

Philadelphia A's to embark on their first season in the fledgling American League. Proceeding straight to the bigs, Plank won 17 games as a rookie. He quickly became the bane both of hitters and umpires. His pitches weren't fancy, but he seemed to take forever between deliveries. Plank claimed he slowed his pace to rattle hitters, and he kept them off balance by talking to himself on the mound.

Plank's achievements were notable. He won 20 or more games in a season seven times for the A's. But because he never led the American League in wins, ERA, or strikeouts, he was never considered the staff ace. He actually rode the bench for the entire 1910 World Series when Mack preferred to go with Jack Coombs and Chief Bender.

After slipping to 15 wins in 1914, Plank deserted the A's to play in the renegade Federal League, so his 300th win came in the uniform of the 1915 St. Louis Terriers. He finished out his career with the St. Louis Browns in 1917, the first southpaw ever to win 300 games. Plank still holds the record for the most wins and most shutouts by an American League portsider. Inducted in 1946.

MAJOR LEAGUE TOTALS			
W	L	ERA	K
326	194	2.35	2,246

◦⚾◦

CLARK GRIFFITH

Clark Calvin Griffith was given the nickname "The Old Fox" while in his 20s. Pitching for Cap Anson's Chicago White Stockings, Griffith was known for having more guile than ability, scuffing and doctoring balls. After a solid pitching career and 20 years as a manager, he purchased the Washington Senators and remained the team's owner for 43 years, until his death. Inducted in 1946.

MAJOR LEAGUE TOTALS			
W	L	ERA	K
237	146	3.31	955

◦⚾◦

BAN JOHNSON

At the urging of his drinking pal, Charles Comiskey, Cincinnati sportswriter Byron Bancroft Johnson assumed control of the Western League, which was weak but had teams in valuable cities. Johnson's leadership proved strong and successful. When the National League contracted from 12 to 8 teams in 1900, the circuit made its move. Renamed the American League, it moved into eastern territories abandoned by the NL, declared itself a major league, and began a series of player raids. When the new league opened in 1901, 111 of the league's 185 players had NL experience. The new league flourished under Johnson, and the National Agreement, signed in 1903, ended the raiding wars between the circuits and established a World Series.

Johnson felt that his founding of the league granted him dictatorial power over its operations. But as the league gained its own momentum, he lost power, his blustery style alienating nearly everybody. Inducted in 1937.

◦⚾◦

JOE TINKER

Joseph Bert Tinker is the least known member of the Chicago Cubs' immortal infield trio in the first decade of the 20th century. Thus, there is a strong temptation to believe he was a lesser player than his two comrades, Johnny Evers and Frank Chance, and probably made the Hall of Fame on their coattails. The truth is that shortstop Tinker was the superior fielder of the three. Inducted in 1946.

MAJOR LEAGUE TOTALS			
BA	H	HR	RBI
.262	1,687	31	782

JOHNNY EVERS

At 5'9", John Joseph Evers was about average height for his time, but he weighed barely 100 pounds when he turned professional in 1902. He was a devout, even fanatical student of the game. His obsession was attributed to his need to gain every extra advantage he could because of his size. Whatever his reason, learning everything there was to know about baseball paid off for Evers. He was the NL MVP in 1914, despite batting just .279. Inducted in 1946.

MAJOR LEAGUE TOTALS			
BA	H	HR	RBI
.270	1,659	12	538

FRANK CHANCE

On the recommendation of former star Cal McVey, Frank Leroy Chance was signed by the Chicago Orphans in 1898 as a backup receiver. Nicknamed "Husk," his size worked against him as he lacked the necessary agility behind the plate.

It took canny manager Frank Selee to switch Chance to first base in 1902. Initially Chance opposed the move, even threatening to quit. He hit .327 in 1903, his first full season as a regular, and then swiped 67 bases the following year to lead the NL and set a modern season record for first basemen. In 1905, Selee named Chance his successor.

Under Chance's guidance, the Cubs won four pennants in the next five years as well as their only two world championships. When the club won a record 116 games in 1906, Chance's nickname of Husk gave way to the name "The Peerless Leader." Inducted in 1946.

MAJOR LEAGUE TOTALS			
BA	H	HR	RBI
.296	1,273	20	596

THREE FINGER BROWN

Three Finger Brown was one of a kind. He became a great pitcher because of rather than in spite of a crippling injury. At the age of 7, Mordecai Peter Centennial Brown accidentally stuck his right hand under a corn chopper, which tore off half his index finger and permanently impaired the thumb and middle finger.

Brown used the damaged hand to his advantage when he pitched. His unnatural grip caused many of his straight pitches to behave like knuckleballs and imparted an extra dip to his curves. The irony is that Brown lacked a major-league fastball and might never have risen above semipro competition were it not for his uncle's corn chopper.

With Brown, the Cubs won four pennants and two World Series between 1906 and 1910. In their victorious 1908 Series, Brown won two games and posted a perfect 0.00 ERA. Inducted in 1949.

MAJOR LEAGUE TOTALS			
W	L	ERA	K
239	130	2.06	1,375

TY COBB

When the first Hall of Fame vote was taken in 1936, Ty Cobb was named on 222 of the 226 ballots cast, to lead all candidates for enshrinement. The shock was not that "The Georgia Peach" outpolled every other player in major-league history, including Babe Ruth and Honus Wagner, but that four voters could ignore Cobb's towering credentials. This slight was understandable only when it is considered that he was not just the greatest player who ever lived—he was also the most despised.

Tyrus Raymond Cobb saw no paradox in that. Throughout his life he contended that he was far from being a great athlete. What made him such a superb player was his unparalleled desire to achieve, to excel, and—above all—to win.

There is no common explanation for the zealous desire he brought to a baseball diamond. With his unquenchable thirst to win and his

Ty Cobb is pictured on the front of "King of Clubs" sheet music.

reckless slides with spikes high whenever he tried to take a base, he was shunned by other players. When he retired in 1928 after 24 seasons in the majors, he held almost every major career and single-season batting and baserunning record. Most have since been broken, owing largely to the longer schedule now played, but one record that almost certainly never will be is his mark for the highest career batting average. Precious few players in the past half century have managed to hit .366 for one season, let alone a 24-year period.

Cobb's deepest regret was that he never played on a World Series winner. His Tigers won consecutive pennants from 1907 to 1909 but always failed in the Series. Although he was only 22 at the time, the 1909 classic was Cobb's last taste of post-season competition.

Whether playing for an also-ran or a contender, though, Cobb gave

the same relentless effort. It was thus difficult to credit a story that surfaced after the 1926 season: Reportedly he and Tris Speaker had helped rig a 1919 game between Detroit and Cleveland. The only part of the story that was consistent with the Cobb everyone knew was that it had been foreordained that Detroit would win the contest. Cobb, not even for all the money in the world, would never have agreed to finish lower than first.

Cobb retired after two seasons with the Philadelphia Athletics, never again to have a full-time job in baseball. He died in Atlanta, Georgia, on July 17, 1961. Inducted in 1936.

MAJOR LEAGUE TOTALS			
BA	H	HR	RBI
.366	4,189	117	1,937

ADDIE JOSS

Addie Joss's career winning percentage of .623 is the highest of any pitcher involved in 200 or more decisions who was never on a pennant winner. Adrian Joss also had the shortest career of any player in the Hall of Fame: He played only nine seasons, all with Cleveland.

His career ERA of 1.89 is second on the all-time list. Joss was, moreover, the most difficult pitcher in history to reach base against. Parsimonious with walks and nearly unhittable when he was on his game, he allowed a record-low 8.73 baserunners per nine innings, excluding errors.

During spring training in 1911, Joss was hospitalized with tubercular meningitis, and on April 14, 1911, he died. His funeral was held on what would have been Opening Day, but his Cleveland teammates refused, en masse, to play that day, attending the funeral instead. Inducted in 1978.

MAJOR LEAGUE TOTALS			
W	L	ERA	K
160	97	1.89	920

CHIEF BENDER

As a member of Connie Mack's Philadelphia A's from 1903 to 1914, Charles Albert Bender was surrounded by fellow All-Star pitchers Eddie Plank and Rube Waddell and backed up by the famous "$100,000 Infield." Pitching for five pennant-

winning teams, Bender won six World Series games in 10 starts, including two apiece in the 1911 and 1913 fall classics.

Bender, half Chippewa Indian, left the White Earth Indian reservation in Minnesota at age 13 to attend school in Philadelphia. He jumped straight from semipro ball to the bigs. He was one of the bigger pitchers of his day at 6'2". Although he didn't rack up many total strikeouts, Bender was often near the top of the AL in strikeouts per game during his stint with the A's. Inducted in 1953.

MAJOR LEAGUE TOTALS			
W	L	ERA	K
212	127	2.46	1,711

ED WALSH

When Edward Augustine Walsh learned to throw a spitball in 1904, he made his already overpowering fastball even tougher to hit.

In 1908, Walsh labored an American League-record 464 innings,

hurled 42 complete games, and became the last pitcher in major-league history to notch 40 victories in a season. Despite his superhuman achievement, the White Sox finished third. The team's problem, a weak attack, was most glaringly in evidence on October 2 when Walsh ceded Cleveland just one run and fanned 15 batters but lost 1-0 because his mates were unable to get a single man on base against Addie Joss. The Joss perfect-game defeat was typical of Walsh's fate all during his career with the White Sox. Inducted in 1946.

MAJOR LEAGUE TOTALS			
W	L	ERA	K
195	126	1.82	1,736

EDDIE COLLINS

John McGraw once said that Eddie Collins was the best ballplayer he'd ever seen. Connie Mack (who managed both Collins and Nap Lajoie) called Collins the best second base-

(continued on page 29)

WALTER JOHNSON

When Walter Johnson joined the Washington Senators in August 1907, they were the worst team in the American League. Then in their seventh year of existence, the Senators had yet to finish higher than sixth place or have a pitcher win 20 games in a season.

Walter Perry Johnson soon remedied the latter shortcoming, but not even his mammoth talents could immediately lift the team out of the nether regions. The Senators finished last or next to last in each of Walter's first five seasons with them even though he twice won 25 games. Then in 1912, Washington vaulted all the way to second place as Johnson stunned with 33 wins, 303 strikeouts, and a 1.39 ERA. When Johnson surpassed belief the following year, winning 36 games and posting a 1.14 ERA, the lowest in American League history by a pitcher with more than 300 innings, the Senators repeated their second-place finish. Eleven years would pass, however, before Washington again returned to contention, and by then Johnson's career seemed at an end. Then 36 years old, he had topped 17 wins in a season for four years.

Those who had written Johnson off, though, were in for a surprise. In 1924, with Washington locked in a season-long battle with the Yankees for the pennant, Johnson paced the junior loop in winning percentage, strikeouts, and ERA. More important, his league-leading 23 wins played an essential role in bringing the Senators their first flag. In the World Series that fall, Johnson was beaten twice by the New York Giants but recovered to win the deciding seventh game in relief. The following season, he spurred Washington to a second consecutive pennant when he was again a 20-game winner. The Pirates, however, proved him mortal in the World Series, topping him in the seventh game after he had twice bested them in earlier rounds.

Johnson was nicknamed "The Big Train" by sportswriter Grant-

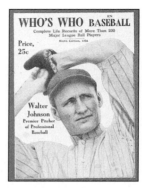

Johnson was featured on the cover of **Who's Who in Baseball** *in 1924.*

land Rice, who compared Walter's size and the velocity of his pitches to an express train. In his 21 years with the Senators, Johnson won 417 games. No other pitcher in this century has equaled this number of wins. More to the point, no one else could have won nearly as many games with the teams for which Johnson played. Except for 1926, when he had little left, Johnson's winning percentage exceeded his team's winning percentage in every season in which he worked 200 or more innings. Most of the time the difference was well over 100 points.

Johnson was one of the first five players elected to the Hall of Fame. Inducted in 1936.

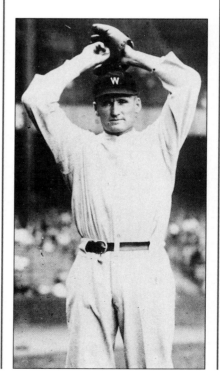

MAJOR LEAGUE TOTALS			
W	L	ERA	K
417	279	2.17	3,509

(continued from page 27)
man he ever saw. Those are strong endorsements coming from two men who saw a lot of baseball. Arguably the greatest second baseman in history, Collins played in 25 seasons and turned in one outstanding season after another for nearly 20 years.

Edward Trowbridge Collins joined Connie Mack's Philadelphia Athletics after graduation. Eddie teamed with Jack Barry at shortstop, Stuffy McInnis at first, and Home Run Baker at third to form the famous "$100,000 Infield." In Collins's first World Series, in 1910, he hit .429 and set four hitting records, after a regular season that included a then-record 81 stolen bases. In all, he won three championships with the A's.

He finished with a .333 lifetime batting average and a .424 career on-base average. He hit over .340 10 times and almost never struck out. Collins owns many fielding records for second basemen, including most assists and total chances. Few have been able to match Collins's abilities and longevity. His

skill at adapting his aggressive style of play to the changing style of baseball may have been his greatest asset. Inducted in 1939.

MAJOR LEAGUE TOTALS			
BA	H	HR	RBI
.333	3,315	47	1,300

BILLY EVANS

Barely age 22 in 1906, William George Evans became the youngest full-time umpire in major-league history. He was the third umpire elected to the Hall of Fame.

In his second umpiring season, Evans nearly died when he was struck in the head by a pop bottle thrown by an irate teenaged fan at a Detroit-St. Louis game. The incident contributed to the eventual banning of bottles at big-league games. Inducted in 1973.

TRIS SPEAKER

Whether Tristram E. Speaker was the greatest fielding center fielder of all time is an argument that can never be finally settled. The statistical evidence shows he was the best outfielder of his era, if not ever, and there is no dispute that he revolutionized outfield play more than any other performer in history. His achievements as a defensive player are so prodigious they can mask the fact that he was also an outstanding hitter. During his career, "The Grey Eagle" topped the junior circuit in

two-base hits a record eight times, amassing 792 doubles, more than any other player in history.

Traded to Cleveland after the 1915 season, Speaker won the bat crown from Ty Cobb. In July 1919, the Indians named Speaker player-manager. Under his guidance, Cleveland shot to second place. In 1920, Cleveland gained its first pennant with Speaker batting .388.

In December 1926, he quit the Indians suddenly, and it emerged that he feared being implicated in an alleged plot to fix a game in 1919 between Detroit and Cleveland with Ty Cobb. The two stars were exonerated, though, when Dutch Leonard, a former pitcher who bore a grudge against both of them, refused to confront the pair in person with his accusations of their crime. Inducted in 1937.

MAJOR LEAGUE TOTALS			
BA	H	HR	RBI
.345	3,514	117	1,529

HOME RUN BAKER

John Franklin Baker received his nickname, "Home Run," when he topped the AL in four-baggers and clubbed two crucial homers for the A's in the 1911 World Series against the New York Giants. Baker was the third baseman in the legendary "$100,000 infield." The 1912 season was Baker's best; he led the AL in both homers and RBI and hit .347, a record for junior circuit third basemen that stood until 1980. Inducted in 1955.

MAJOR LEAGUE TOTALS			
BA	H	HR	RBI
.307	1,838	96	987

RUBE MARQUARD

Richard William "Rube" Marquard joined the Giants' pitching staff as an 18-year-old rookie in 1908 and exploded in 1911. Rube went 24-7 that year, leading the league in winning percentage and strikeouts. Teamed with ace Christy Mathewson, Marquard led the Giants to the first of three consecutive pennants. In those three years, Marquard won 73 games (including 19 straight in 1912) and lost just 28. Inducted in 1971.

MAJOR LEAGUE TOTALS			
W	L	ERA	K
201	177	3.08	1,593

RUBE FOSTER

Andrew "Rube" Foster earned himself the title, "Father of Black Baseball." An outstanding pitcher, Foster was a big man with a big fastball. Pitching for the Leland Giants in Chicago in 1909, Foster wrested control of the team from owner Frank Leland. He led the renamed American Giants to prominence as the top black team in the country.

In 1919, with a substantial, sustained effort and much of his own money, Foster formed the Negro National League, an eight-team league with seven black owners. Foster had a dream, which he drummed into the heads of his players. He wanted them to play at a high level of excellence so they would be ready when integration finally came. The effort finally got to Foster: In 1926, he was taken to an asylum after a spate of erratic behavior. He died in 1930; his funeral drawing an immense crowd. Inducted in 1981.

HARRY HOOPER

Harry Hooper is the only outfielder elected to the Hall of Fame primarily because of his defensive skills. Although he had 2,466 hits and was an excellent leadoff batter with good speed, Hooper was never a league leader in a single major offensive department. He was an important cog on four Red Sox world championship teams during the 1910s. Inducted in 1971.

MAJOR LEAGUE TOTALS			
BA	H	HR	RBI
.281	2,466	75	817

ZACH WHEAT

The Brooklyn Dodgers' fortunes brightened in 1909 when Zachariah Davis Wheat joined them. For the next 17 years, Wheat occupied left field. By the time he left the team after 1926, he held almost every existing Dodger career offensive

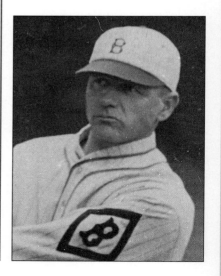

record. Only three of his marks—for runs, home runs, and stolen bases—were subsequently broken.

Wheat played for his first pennant-winning team in 1916 and topped the NL in slugging average and total bases. Two years later, Wheat led the senior loop in batting with the fewest total bases ever by a hit-crown winner with more than 400 at bats, and was the last batting leader in NL history to go homerless for a season. When Babe Ruth came along, Wheat joined in the increased offensive output, regularly posting home run totals in double figures. Inducted in 1959.

MAJOR LEAGUE TOTALS			
BA	H	HR	RBI
.317	2,884	132	1,248

RAY SCHALK

Raymond William Schalk's career batting average of .253 is the lowest of any position player in the Hall of Fame. He was selected in recognition of his outstanding defense. He caught 100 or more games for 11 straight seasons at one point in his career, a major-league record at the time. As a member of the 1919 White Sox, Schalk tried valiantly to thwart the fixers. Inducted in 1955.

MAJOR LEAGUE TOTALS			
BA	H	HR	RBI
.253	1,345	11	594

POP LLOYD

John Henry "Pop" Lloyd first jumped from semipro baseball to the black professional leagues in 1905 at age 21, and was a good enough player to play semipro until age 58. A very good defensive shortstop for most of the early days in his career, he also showcased a line-drive stroke that drove his average to dizzying heights. Lloyd played for whatever team could pay him. He played for various Philadelphia teams, on New York and New Jersey teams, and with the Chicago American Giants, among others.

Lloyd was often likened to Honus Wagner, a comparison Wagner was proud to acknowledge. It was an apt analogy, because like Wagner, Lloyd was highly regarded, was a terrific hitter, and was known to scoop up dirt and pebbles along with ground balls. Inducted in 1977.

SAM RICE

By the time Senators skipper Clark Griffith gave Edgar Charles Rice a job in the Washington outfield late in 1916, Rice was already past 26 years old. It seemed unlikely he would wind up playing 20 years in the majors, let alone compile more hits than any other player in Washington history, particularly since he missed most of the 1918 season while serving in the Army. Upon returning to the Senators in 1919 at age 29, with only one full season as a regular under his belt, Rice

embarked on a tear that left him only 13 hits short of the hallowed 3,000 total when he retired.

Rice's prime years were in the middle 1920s. During a four-year span he led the American League twice in hits and once in triples. Additionally, he played on Washington's first two pennant-winning teams in 1924 and 1925. Inducted in 1963.

MAJOR LEAGUE TOTALS			
BA	H	HR	RBI
.322	2,987	34	1,078

MAX CAREY

Almost from the day Maximilian Carnarius joined the Pittsburgh Pirates, Honus Wagner took him under his wing, advising him to keep his legs in shape, believing that speed was the tool with which Carey would make his mark. He became a scientific basestealer who mastered his craft by diligently studying pitchers and learning their pickoff moves. Carey was a fixture in the Pittsburgh outfield for 16 years. Inducted in 1961.

MAJOR LEAGUE TOTALS			
BA	H	HR	RBI
.285	2,665	70	800

GROVER ALEXANDER

When the Phillies acquired Grover Cleveland Alexander for $750 in 1911, they became contenders. In 1911, "Pete" won 28 games. In 1915, his 31 wins led the Phillies to their only pennant before 1950. The next season, he scored a personal-high 33 victories and notched an all-time-record 16 shutouts. When he won 30 again in 1917, he became the last 30-game winner in two straight seasons, let alone three.

He lost the hearing in one ear during World War I and began experiencing the first symptoms of epilepsy. Between illness and shell shock, Alexander came to rely more and more on alcohol.

As a Cardinal in the 1926 World Series, Alexander won both the second and sixth games in a starting role and then went out on the town, believing his work was done. But in Game 7, when the Yanks loaded the bases in the seventh inning with two out, Alexander was called out of the bullpen to protect a 3-2 lead. Despite a monumental hangover, he proceeded to fan rookie slugging sensation Tony Lazzeri on four pitches. Alexander then set down the vaunted New Yorkers in the final two innings without surrendering a hit. Inducted in 1938.

MAJOR LEAGUE TOTALS			
W	L	ERA	K
373	208	2.56	2,198

CONNIE MACK

Cornelius Alexander Mack (born McGillicuddy) had the longest baseball career ever—64 years as a player and manager, starting in the 19th century and lasting through the first half of the 20th.

Western League commissioner Ban Johnson invited Mack to pilot the Milwaukee franchise. In 1901, when Johnson elevated the status of the minor circuit to the major AL, he gave the Philly franchise to Connie. Mack remained the A's manager through the 1950 season.

Mack built a championship club around Eddie Plank, Rube Waddell, and Chief Bender, winning pennants in 1902 and 1905. Behind hurlers Bender and Jack Coombs

and the "$100,000 infield," the A's won three world championships (1910, '11, and '13).

When the Federal League began to raid the two established leagues, Mack watched his team unravel. Selling off his best players, he doomed the club to a record seven straight last-place finishes.

Mack's method was to buy hot prospects from the minor-league teams, trusting his ability to discover stars. In the mid-1920s, Mack's charges were usually in pennant races. By 1929, the A's exploded. Young stars such as Al Simmons, Jimmie Foxx, Mickey Cochrane, and Lefty Grove won three straight pennants and the World Series in 1929 and 1930. Then Mack sold many of his best players to better-heeled teams and wallowed in the second division for the rest of his career. Inducted in 1937.

MAJOR LEAGUE TOTALS		
W	L	PCT
3,731	3,948	.486

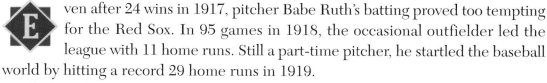

Even after 24 wins in 1917, pitcher Babe Ruth's batting proved too tempting for the Red Sox. In 95 games in 1918, the occasional outfielder led the league with 11 home runs. Still a part-time pitcher, he startled the baseball world by hitting a record 29 home runs in 1919.

When Red Sox owner Harry Frazee needed funds to underwrite his theater productions, he sold Ruth to the Yankees. Nine months later—thanks to the cozy dimensions of the Polo Grounds, the new cork-centered ball, and the banning of the spitball—Ruth swatted 54 home runs. His .378 average, 59 homers, and 171 runs batted in of 1921 emphasized that baseball's nature had changed. The slugger's popularity had boomed in direct proportion to his bat, and the fans flocked to the ballpark to see Ruth play, both in New York and on the road. After the Black Sox fiasco, the Babe lifted the game back to its spot as the nation's pastime.

When they saw how well Ruth and the Yankees were drawing, the baseball owners decided to gear the game toward offense. By the end of the 1920s, such sluggers as Lou Gehrig, Mel Ott, and Jimmie Foxx were featured. In 1930, a souped-up ball in the NL inflated batting figures so wildly that it had to be deadened a year later. Eleven players on the pennant-winning Cardinals hit .300, and even the last-place Phillies hit .315, not enough to compensate for a record 6.71 team ERA. While pitchers eventually lessened the gap, baseball had survived the Depression.

Above: The makeshift knots in the webbing of Frankie Frisch's favorite glove are a testimony to Frisch's fondness for the fielding tool and to the longevity gloves enjoyed in his day.

STAN COVALESKI

Although he toiled in the minor leagues for eight seasons and was nearly 27 years old before joining Cleveland in 1916, Stanley Covaleski won 20 or more games for four straight years between 1918 and 1921. Overshadowed by 31-game winner Jim Bagby in 1920 when Cleveland won its first pennant, Covaleski emerged as the team's hero that autumn when he registered three World Series victories against the Brooklyn Dodgers. In 1925, he led the American League in winning percentage while helping the Senators to their second consecutive pennant. Inducted in 1969.

MAJOR LEAGUE TOTALS			
W	L	ERA	K
215	142	2.89	981

JOHN MCGRAW

John McGraw was the most controversial, notorious, hateful, inspiring manager in baseball history and the winningest manager in National League history.

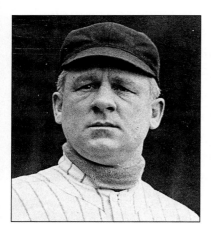

John Joseph McGraw played in an era when rowdyism was rampant, and he was among the worst offenders, battling with opponents, umpires, and fans for any edge. His infamous Baltimore Oriole club twice won the Temple Cup. He jumped to the nascent American League in 1901 but didn't get along with AL founder Ban Johnson. Through some conniving, he wound up managing the Giants at age 29, and he managed the team for the next 30 years.

The Giants won pennants in 1904 and 1905. There was no World Series in 1904, as Orioles owner John Brush and McGraw scoffed at the American League. In 1905, the Giants beat Philadelphia for the first of McGraw's three world championships, though he lost six World Series throughout his long career. "Little Napoleon" brought three pennants from 1911 to 1913 and then won another in 1917. A fine field general who knew all the tricks for manufacturing runs in that low-scoring era, he was the "absolute czar" of the team, relying on discipline and fear. His violent nature often got him into trouble both off the field and on.

McGraw built a powerhouse in the early 1920s, winning a record four straight pennants from 1921 to 1924, with World Series victories in 1921 and 1922. The '24 pennant was his last. Inducted in 1937.

MAJOR LEAGUE TOTALS		
W	L	PCT
2,763	1,948	.586

BILL KLEM

William Joseph Klem umpired in the National League for a record 37 years. Recognized early on as the best arbiter in baseball, he continued to work only behind the plate for 16 years, even after more umpires were added. During his long career, Klem officiated in a record 18 World Series, the last of which was in 1940. Inducted in 1953.

HERB PENNOCK

Herb Pennock was another of Connie Mack's discoveries, a terrific left-hander who would eventually become the best-remembered pitcher of Babe Ruth's Yankees. Pennock was age 29 and barely a .500 pitcher when he arrived in the Bronx, but in his first season there, he led the league in winning percentage at .760 (19-6). He went on to two 20-win seasons for the Yankees and a 162-90 record in 11 seasons. Inducted in 1948.

MAJOR LEAGUE TOTALS			
W	L	ERA	K
241	162	3.60	1,227

RABBIT MARANVILLE

Walter James Vincent Maranville was nicknamed "Rabbit" by fans who loved the way the diminutive shortstop scurried and hopped about the infield. At 5'5½" and 155 pounds, Maranville is the smallest 20th-century player in the Hall of Fame. It was his glove and his leadership that made his reputation, and in these respects he had few peers.

Renowned for his impulsive and zany off-the-field antics, Rabbit was a star for the "Miracle Braves" of 1914. Traded to Pittsburgh following the 1920 season, he continued his carousing along with his spectacular defense. Appointed player-manager of the Cubs in July 1925, he wore out his welcome after only eight weeks and was fired. Idled most of the 1926 season by an injury, he was banished to the minors in 1927. The pink slip so shocked Maranville that he stopped drinking. By the end of the season he had been recalled by the Cardinals, and he played through 1935. Inducted in 1954.

MAJOR LEAGUE TOTALS			
BA	H	HR	RBI
.258	2,605	28	884

EPPA RIXEY

Before Warren Spahn, Eppa Rixey held the National League record for the most career wins by a left-

hander with 266. Although he stood 6'5" and weighed 210 pounds, Rixey was anything but a fireballer; his strong point was control and keeping hitters off balance.

In 1916, Rixey won 22 games, and with Pete Alexander, gave the Phils the best lefty-righty duo in the game. When Alexander was traded to the Cubs after the 1917 season, the Phils plummeted in the standings. To his relief, Rixey was traded to Cincinnati just before the 1921 season.

Rixey toiled for 13 years with the Reds, three times winning 20 or more games in a season. His pinnacle came in 1922, when his 25 victories paced the National League. Rixey remained one of the mainstays of the Reds mound staff through the 1920s. In 1969, he was voted the greatest left-handed pitcher in Reds history. Inducted in 1963.

MAJOR LEAGUE TOTALS			
W	L	ERA	K
266	251	3.15	1,350

MILLER HUGGINS

In 1913, Miller James Huggins was named manager of the Cards after Roger Bresnahan was fired. Under Hug's leadership, the Cardinals rose to third place in 1914, the highest finish ever by a St. Louis team in the NL to that point. Hired to manage the Yankees in 1918, Huggins recommended they obtain Babe Ruth in 1920. The rest is history: six

pennants and three Series titles in eight years. Inducted in 1964.

MAJOR LEAGUE TOTALS		
W	L	PCT
1,413	1,134	.555

EDD ROUSH

Edd J. Roush kept himself in shape, so he had no use for spring training and was almost always a holdout. But that didn't keep him from hitting success: He won his first National League batting crown in 1917 after a spring holdout. The next year Roush missed the title by .002, but won again in 1919. In 1923 he didn't sign until July, but still swatted .351 for the season. Inducted in 1962.

MAJOR LEAGUE TOTALS			
BA	H	HR	RBI
.323	2,376	68	981

HARRY HEILMANN

Harry Heilmann was the last right-handed batter in the American League to hit over .400. Had he made just one more hit in 1927 and four more hits in both 1921 and 1925, he would have been the only player in major-league history to top the .400 mark four times. As it was, he won four AL batting titles and became the first player to hit at least one home run in every major-league park during his career. Yet,

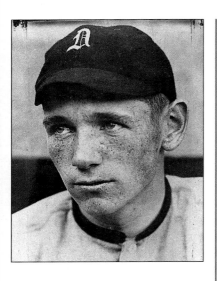

WILBERT ROBINSON

A great catcher and batsman for the old Baltimore Orioles, Wilbert Robinson found himself at the center of baseball's liveliest rivalry when he split from his old pal John McGraw of the Giants to manage the Brooklyn team. Before his first year in Brooklyn was out, Robinson had been nicknamed "Uncle Robbie" and sportswriters had begun calling his team the "Robins." Brooklyn fans called him a genius after he brought home pennants in 1916 and 1920. Inducted in 1945.

MAJOR LEAGUE TOTALS		
W	L	PCT
1,399	1,398	.500

RED FABER

Urban Charles "Red" Faber was a White Sox pitcher on two pennant-winning teams, 1917 and 1919. But various ailments kept him out of the 1919 World Series. Had Red been healthy, there might never have been a Black Sox scandal. Faber would win 20 or more games in each of the next three seasons, but the White Sox never finished higher than fifth in Faber's remaining 13 years with them. Inducted in 1964.

GEORGE SISLER

George Sisler was one of the best first baseman who ever played the game, despite performing at peak capacity for only about half of his career. He amply demonstrated, however, that he may well have been the greatest hitter of them all.

Like Babe Ruth, George Harold Sisler began his career as a pitcher. Shortly after joining St. Louis, Sisler beat Walter Johnson in a classic pitcher's duel. Stationed at first base in 1916, Sisler hit .305 in his first full season. After three successive seasons in which he batted around .350, Sisler went wild in 1920. Not only did he top the American League with a .407 average, but he collected an all-time-record 257 hits and set a new 20th-century mark for first basemen with 19 home runs.

Two years later, Sisler again cracked the .400 barrier when he soared to .420. Since he also paced the AL in runs, hits, and triples, he (continued on page 38)

for all his accomplishments, Heilmann was not elected to the Hall of Fame until 1952, the winter after his death. Critics claimed that his .342 career batting average was inflated because he played during the 1920s, when astronomical averages were the norm.

Heilmann first topped the .300 barrier in 1919 when he posted a .320 average with 93 RBI for Detroit. The next season new Detroit manager Ty Cobb spent considerable time tutoring Heilmann at the plate, which paid dividends when he won the AL batting title in 1921, a feat he repeated every other season for the next six years (1923, 1925, and 1927). He also had more than 200 base hits in each of the four years that he won the hit crown. Inducted in 1952.

MAJOR LEAGUE TOTALS			
BA	H	HR	RBI
.342	2,660	183	1,539

MAJOR LEAGUE TOTALS			
W	L	ERA	K
254	213	3.15	1,471

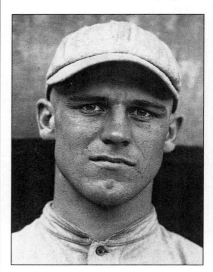

BABE RUTH

I n 1917, when George Herman Ruth was 22 years old, he was 6′2″, a slim 180 pounds of muscle, and a superb left-handed pitcher with a lifetime record of 67-34. His prowess with the bat, however, prompted the Red Sox manager to cut in half the number of starts of his young ace in 1918 and give him 317 at bats playing as a regular out-fielder. He went 13-7 pitching and led the league with 11 homers. The kid was the talk of both leagues.

Sold to the New York Yankees before the 1920 season, Ruth took New York, baseball, and America by storm. His 54 home runs were more than any other American League team total. His .847 slug-ging average still stands as the sin-gle-season record, and he hit .376 with a league-leading 158 runs and 137 RBI. He dominated the AL almost up to his 1935 retirement: a batting title in 1924, 12 home run titles, and eight times leading the

Babe's roommate once said, "I don't room with Babe. I room with his suitcase."

league in runs, six times in RBI, and 13 times in slugging. He might have won more honors, but a 1922 suspension for barnstorming and a 1925 intestinal abscess cost him nearly 100 games. The Bambino never struck out 100 times in a sea-son, and he led the league in walks 11 times, including a record 170 in 1923. He still holds lifetime marks in walks and slugging. He led the way for a new, high-offense game that packed in fans in record num-bers and helped heal the wounds left by the 1919 Black Sox scandal.

The Babe led the Yankees to seven World Series appearances and four championships. He teamed with Lou Gehrig to form the most feared one-two punch in baseball history, and in 1927 the fabled "Murderer's Row" of the Yankees won 110 games and lost just 44. Ruth set a record that year

that was to capture the imagination like no other, hitting 60 home runs in a single season.

Beyond his on-field heroics, Ruth—one of the first five players inducted into the Hall of Fame in 1936—was a legend for his off-the-field adventures as well. His lust for life equaled his lust for homers. He made friends everywhere—while he ate everything, drank every-thing, tried everything. He was the most beloved player ever to play the game. The Hall of Fame was created for players like Babe Ruth. He died in 1948 of throat cancer. Inducted in 1936.

MAJOR LEAGUE TOTALS			
BA	H	HR	RBI
.342	2,873	714	2,213

(continued from page 36)
became the natural choice for the league's MVP Award. Despite Sisler's heroics, the Browns still could not land their first pennant, losing to the Yankees by a single-game margin. Sisler finished his career without ever appearing in a World Series.

Infected sinuses began to affect Sisler's vision in 1922, and he never again rose to the heights his talent had promised. Inducted in 1939.

MAJOR LEAGUE TOTALS			
BA	H	HR	RBI
.340	2,812	102	1,175

DAVE BANCROFT

As a key member of John McGraw's Giants, David James "Beauty" Bancroft batted second behind George Burns, one of the best leadoff men around. With outstanding hitters following him, Bancroft saw good pitches and blossomed at the plate. It was with his glove at short, however, that Bancroft made his reputation. In 1922, he topped the senior circuit in both putouts and assists and set a major-league record that still stands by accepting 984 fielding chances. Inducted in 1971.

MAJOR LEAGUE TOTALS			
BA	H	HR	RBI
.279	2,004	32	591

GEORGE KELLY

George Lange Kelly was a key player in the last glory years of John McGraw's Giants, helping win four straight pennants from 1921 to 1924 and two world championships. Kelly was a good first baseman, and a good enough fielder to play more than 100 games at second base in 1925 when Bill Terry was stationed at first base. Kelly led the league in fielding categories 12 times. Inducted in 1973.

MAJOR LEAGUE TOTALS			
BA	H	HR	RBI
.297	1,778	148	1,020

ROGERS HORNSBY

Rogers Hornsby was the greatest right-handed hitter in history. With the exception of Ty Cobb, no superstar was more disliked than Hornsby. Aloof, independent, and brutally honest, he may be the least understood great player.

Hornsby hit .313 for St. Louis as a rookie and played a surprisingly adequate shortstop. In 1917, his second full season, he topped the National League in slugging and was second in batting. Hornsby slipped below .300 for the only time in his career in 1918 but continued to rank high in all slugging departments. Moved to third base in 1919, "The Rajah" again finished second in league batting. The following spring, Hornsby took the batting and RBI crowns in his first

season as a second baseman. His .370 average was the highest in the 20th century by an NL second sacker.

No one expected Hornsby to duplicate that figure in 1921, and he did not. Instead he hit .397 and then followed up by hitting .401 in 1922, .384 in 1923, .424 (the 20th-century major-league record) in 1924, and .403 in 1925 to make him the only player in history to average over .400 for a five-year span. During the 1920s, Hornsby hit below .361 on just one occasion. That came in 1926 after he was made player-manager of the Cardinals. The dual responsibility held him to a .317 mark, but his Cardinals won their first NL pennant that year. Inducted in 1942.

MAJOR LEAGUE TOTALS			
BA	H	HR	RBI
.358	2,930	301	1,584

OSCAR CHARLESTON

Oscar Charleston put punch in the lineups of no less than a dozen teams in his 35-year career. He was a barrel-chested man of great strength, a long-hitter who could hit for average and run like the wind. Only Josh Gibson, the memory of whom is fresher, challenges Charleston's reputation as a slugger, and only Cool Papa Bell is mentioned with him when the best center fielders of the Negro Leagues are named.

John B. Holway wrote "there were three things Oscar Charleston excelled at on the field: hitting, fielding, and fighting. He loved all three, and it's a toss-up which he was best at." Each of the three is documented. Charleston's lifetime average is .353. Newt Allen said "He hit so hard, he'd knock gloves off you." Charleston's 11 homers

against major-league pitchers in exhibition games ties for the highest total recorded, and he hit them for distance, too. In the field, Charleston was just as impressive, with an arm more accurate than strong and the speed to run down drives in any part of the park easily. Right fielder Dave Malarcher, who played alongside Charleston, said: "He could play all the outfield. I just caught foul balls. I stayed on the lines." His spectacular catches are legendary. Inducted in 1976.

BURLEIGH GRIMES

When Burleigh Arland Grimes won his 270th game in 1934, it was not only his final victory, it was also the last game in major-league history won by a pitcher legally permitted to throw a spitball. His spitball was among the most effective ever, often breaking some seven or eight inches. Inducted in 1964.

MAJOR LEAGUE TOTALS			
W	L	ERA	K
270	212	3.53	1,512

ROSS YOUNGS

John McGraw called Royce Middlebrook Youngs "the greatest outfielder I ever saw," and "Pep" was a fixture on McGraw's four-straight pennant-winning teams of 1921 to 1924. He was a prototypical McGraw star: a fast, high-average hitter who had little power but

played great defense. Youngs had a fearsome arm, leading loop right fielders in assists three times. Inducted in 1972.

MAJOR LEAGUE TOTALS			
BA	H	HR	RBI
.322	1,491	42	592

WAITE HOYT

Waite Charles Hoyt labored in the major leagues for 21 years, pitching in six World Series and five championships with the Yankees. In his first season there, Hoyt won 19 games, helping New York to its first AL pennant. In that year's nine-game World Series, he won twice in three games while not allowing a single run in his 27 innings. It was the first of three straight pennants for the Yanks. Inducted in 1969.

MAJOR LEAGUE TOTALS			
W	L	ERA	K
237	182	3.59	1,206

JESSE HAINES

Jesse Haines served a St. Louis Cardinals-record 18-year stint on the mound, surprising since he was 27 years old before he became a regular pitcher in the major leagues. A three-time 20-game winner, he did some of his best work in World Series competition. Haines relied on a blistering fastball and a baffling knuckleball that he learned

from Athletics ace Eddie Rommell. Inducted in 1970.

MAJOR LEAGUE TOTALS			
W	L	ERA	K
210	158	3.64	981

JUDY JOHNSON

Of the Negro League Hall of Famers, William Julius Johnson has perhaps the weakest batting stats. His fielding at third base is usually described as steady or intelligent rather than spectacular. Yet everyone who played with him or saw him play agreed he was a great ballplayer.

He joined one of the powerhouse teams in the east, the Philadelphia Hilldales, in 1921. He was a line-drive hitter who drove in a high number of runs despite not hitting a large number of homers. Johnson played for Philadelphia for 11 years and played winter ball in Cuba. He hit a career-high .406 in

1929, a year in black baseball that matched white baseball in 1930 for unprecedented offensive totals. He was chosen MVP by sportswriter Rollo Wilson for the season.

Johnson became a member of perhaps the best Negro Leagues team in history when he joined Gus Greenlee's Pittsburgh Crawfords in 1932. Greenlee built the first stadium completely owned by an African American. To fill his new ballpark, Greenlee sought the best talent he could find, raiding the Pittsburgh-based Homestead Grays and other teams for the best black players money could buy. Managed by Oscar Charleston, the Crawfords boasted the talents of Josh Gibson, Satchel Paige, and Cool Papa Bell. Johnson finished his playing career with the Crawfords in 1938. Inducted in 1975.

FRANKIE FRISCH

Frank Francis Frisch had a competitive drive that made him a natural leader on the field. John McGraw recognized the talents of "The Fordham Flash" and brought him to the Giants in 1919. In 1921, the Giants won the first of four straight pennants.

In 1923, he led the league with 223 hits, establishing himself as one of the great stars of the day. An exceptional fielder, Frisch was called "possibly the flashiest second baseman of any day." Moving to St. Louis with the famous "Gashouse Gang," he appeared in four World Series, winning one in 1931 and

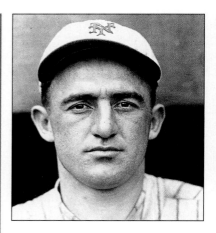

leading the team to another in 1934, a year after becoming player-manager. Well-respected by his contemporaries, Frisch won the first MVP Award in the National League in 1931, after a year that was not his best. He managed for 16 years, with St. Louis, Pittsburgh, and Chicago, winning 1,138 games. Inducted in 1947.

MAJOR LEAGUE TOTALS			
BA	H	HR	RBI
.316	2,880	105	1,244

KENESAW MOUNTAIN LANDIS

The headline in *The New York Times* in 1920 read "BASEBALL PEACE DECLARED; LANDIS NAMED DICTATOR." Over a decade later, in legal court documents, he was called "legally an absolute despot." Judge Kenesaw Mountain Landis was more than the owners who hired him bargained for: a tough, uncompromis-

ing man who trusted his own opinion beyond any other. Landis was rarely photographed smiling, and the stern, craggy eccentric captured in his photos seems to have been a true picture of the man.

Landis is best known for his rulings concerning the 1919 Black Sox, when he banned the eight players accused of throwing World Series games from baseball despite the lack of evidence to convict them in a court of law. He also put an end to barnstorming by making an example of Babe Ruth. Landis suspended Ruth and two others for 40 days in 1922. Inducted in 1944.

PIE TRAYNOR

Harold Joseph "Pie" Traynor floundered as a rookie Pirate shortstop in 1922 for nearly two months until Bill McKecknie was installed as the Pittsburgh manager. One of McKecknie's first moves was to switch Traynor to third base. Pie hit .282 that season. In 1923, he hit .338 and led NL third sackers in putouts and assists. The Bucs won the pen-

nant in 1925, with Traynor hitting .320 with 106 RBI, leading again in defense.

In 1927, Traynor hit .342 and had 106 RBI, again leading the loop in putouts, as Pittsburgh again took the pennant. Over the next four years, Pie's lowest batting average was .337 in 1928, and he slugged 100-plus RBI over a five-year stretch.

Traynor played with the Pirates his entire 17-year career and also managed the club for five and one-half seasons. In 1969, he was selected as the game's all-time greatest third baseman by sportswriters. Inducted in 1948.

MAJOR LEAGUE TOTALS			
BA	H	HR	RBI
.320	2,416	58	1,273

JOE SEWELL

Joseph Wheeler Sewell was a steady .300 hitter, although he was active during a high-average era. But he almost never struck out. The

holder of every major season and career record for fewest whiffs, he fanned only 114 times in 14 seasons and 7,132 at bats, an average of only one strikeout for every 63 plate trips. During his peak years, Sewell was also the best fielding shortstop in the game. Inducted in 1977.

MAJOR LEAGUE TOTALS			
BA	H	HR	RBI
.312	2,226	49	1,055

KIKI CUYLER

Hazen Shirley "Kiki" Cuyler debuted as a Pirate in 1924 with one of the finest rookie seasons ever. He batted .354, fourth highest in the league, cracked 16 triples, and swiped 32 bases. When Cuyler hiked his average to .357 and led the loop in both triples and runs as a sophomore, he was hailed as the game's newest star.

Unfortunately, even though he had a fine career, Cuyler never again ascended to the heights

he reached early on. His critics believed he had the talent to be as good as any player in the game but lacked the necessary drive to excel. The Pirates grew disenchanted with Kiki midway through the 1927 season and benched him in the World Series that fall. Two months later he was traded. Cuyler enjoyed several banner seasons with the Cubs. Inducted in 1968.

MAJOR LEAGUE TOTALS			
BA	H	HR	RBI
.321	2,299	128	1,065

GOOSE GOSLIN

Goose Goslin was the only American Leaguer between 1921 and 1939 to play on five pennant-winning teams despite never playing for the Yankees or under Connie Mack.

Nicknamed Goose both because of his last name and because of his large nose, Leon Allen Goslin quickly emerged as a standout slugger. In 1923, he led the American League in triples. A year later he was the loop's RBI king, his 129 ribbies topping even Babe Ruth and preventing the Babe from winning a Triple Crown.

The Senators took back-to-back pennants in 1924 and 1925. Goslin was dealt to the Browns early in the 1930 season only a year and a half after he won the AL batting title. Washington reobtained him on December 14, 1932. He helped the Senators win their third and last

pennant the next summer. Swapped to Detroit, Goslin played on flag winners in each of his first two seasons there. Inducted in 1968.

MAJOR LEAGUE TOTALS			
BA	H	HR	RBI
.316	2,735	248	1,609

DAZZY VANCE

No player in the Hall of Fame took longer to make his mark in the major leagues than Clarence Arthur "Dazzy" Vance. After ten years in the minors, he joined the Dodgers in 1922 at age 31 (although he claimed he was two years younger). Vance won 18 games in his first full big-league test and topped the National League in strikeouts for the first of seven consecutive seasons. Inducted in 1955.

MAJOR LEAGUE TOTALS			
W	L	ERA	K
197	140	3.24	2,045

JIM BOTTOMLEY

James LeRoy Bottomley was known as "Sunny Jim" because of his disposition, but he was no friend to enemy pitchers, as he posted a .310 career average, 2,313 hits, and 1,422 RBI. He replaced Cardinal first baseman Jack Fournier in 1923 and held the position for 10 years. Besides Bottomley's .367 average in 1925, he smacked 227 hits with a league-leading 44 doubles and 128 RBI. In 1925, Bottomley began a string of five straight seasons of over 120 RBI. Inducted in 1974.

MAJOR LEAGUE TOTALS			
BA	H	HR	RBI
.310	2,313	219	1,422

GABBY HARTNETT

Until Johnny Bench, Charles Leo "Gabby" Hartnett was known as the greatest catcher in the history of the National League. A prototypical catcher, he couldn't run, would talk your ear off—they didn't call him Gabby for nothing—and lasted for years on a lot of bat and a lot more savvy.

When Hartnett took over as Cub catcher in 1924, he held the position until the late 1930s, save for an injury-plagued 1929. Gabby became a reliable stickman, batting in the .275 range with some power. After an arm injury in 1929, he exploded in 1930, hitting .339 with 37 homers and 122 RBI.

(continued on page 44)

LOU GEHRIG

On May 31, 1925, Lou Gehrig pinch-hit for Pee Wee Wanninger. The next day, regular Yank first baseman Wally Pipp sat down with a headache, and the next day, when backup first sacker Fred Merkle seemed about to collapse from the heat, manager Miller Huggins brought in Gehrig as a late-inning replacement. Merkle never started another game in the majors and Pipp never got his job back. Gehrig played a record 2,130 consecutive games for the Yankees, a record many said was unbreakable. Gehrig was the best all-around first baseman in baseball history.

Henry Louis Gehrig spent two seasons in the minors. But in his first full season, he hit .295, scored 73 runs, and knocked home 68 teammates—the last time he tallied fewer than 100 runs or collected fewer than 100 RBI in a full season. Gehrig averaged the highest number of runs and RBI per game of any 20th-century player.

In 1931, Gehrig set an AL record with 184 RBI, breaking his own mark of 175. The next year, he became the first player in the 20th century to clout four home runs in a game. An excellent baserunner and a solid first baseman, he was the AL's MVP twice.

In 1934, Gehrig won the Triple Crown while copping his only batting title with a .363 mark. Two years later, he garnered his final home run crown with 49, tying his own personal high. When Gehrig's batting average slipped to .295 in 1938 and his RBI and homer totals

Gehrig was featured on the April 1935 issue of **Baseball Magazine.**

also dipped, it seemed just an off year. The strange slump persisted into the next season. When teammates began congratulating him for making routine plays, Lou knew the time had come to step down. On May 2, 1939, he took himself out of the lineup for the first time in nearly 14 years. A few weeks later, tests revealed he had amyotrophic lateral sclerosis, a rare, always fatal disease. Knowing he would soon die, Gehrig retired formally on July 4, 1939, where he tearfully told a packed Yankee Stadium, "Today, I consider myself the luckiest man on the face of the earth." When Lou Gehrig left baseball, he had 493 home runs, second at the time only to Babe Ruth. Inducted in 1939.

MAJOR LEAGUE TOTALS			
BA	H	HR	RBI
.340	2,721	493	1,995

(continued from page 42)

In 1935, Hartnett was named National League MVP, though his power stats would not stand with those of the heavy hitters of his day. His .344 average was third in the league, and he led league receivers in assists, double plays, and fielding average as he guided Cub pitchers to 100 wins and a pennant. His last three years with the Cubs were as player-manager.

Hartnett is best known for the "Homer in the Gloamin'" in 1938. As player-manager of the Cubs, he led his team from nine games out in August to wrest the pennant away from the Pirates, blasting a home run with the score tied and two out in the ninth inning. Inducted in 1955.

MAJOR LEAGUE TOTALS			
BA	H	HR	RBI
.297	1,912	236	1,179

COOL PAPA BELL

James Thomas Bell was a switch-hitter with the speed to beat out ground balls and to score from second on fly-outs. He also possessed the power to hit the long ball right-handed. He was widely recognized as the fastest man in baseball, and long-time teammate Satchel Paige said Bell could turn out the light and be in bed before the room got dark.

Bell was with the St. Louis Stars for 10 seasons. He gained his fame with the great Pittsburgh Crawfords team and, later, with the Homestead Grays. He joined the Crawfords in 1933, playing alongside future Hall of Famers Satchel Paige, Oscar Charleston, Judy Johnson, and Josh Gibson. Other very good players—Sam Bankhead, Sam Streeter, Rap Dixon, Cy Perkins, Leroy Matlock, and Vic Harris—also played for the Crawfords. It may have been the greatest concentration of talent in baseball at the time.

Bell's lifetime average, by available records, was .338, and he hit .392 in exhibition games against major-leaguers. He once stole more than 175 bases in a 200-game season, but as Bell remembered, "One day I got five hits and stole five bases, but none of that was written down because they didn't bring the scorebook to the game that day." Inducted in 1974.

TRAVIS JACKSON

After leading the league in errors in 1924, Travis Calvin Jackson became one of the best fielders in the league, earning the nickname "Stonewall."

Blessed with a very strong arm, Jackson became a regular league-leader in assists and double plays and was voted the outstanding major-league shortstop by *The Sporting News* in 1927, 1928, and 1929. Inducted in 1982.

MAJOR LEAGUE TOTALS			
BA	H	HR	RBI
.291	1,768	135	929

BILL FOSTER

William Hendrick Foster, half-brother of Hall-of-Famer Rube Foster, was the epitome of the canny lefty. Hurling for six different teams in his 15-year Negro League career, he baffled hitters with a dazzling assortment of pitches. The secret was that he threw them all with exactly the same motion. Foster was the pitcher managers wanted in a big game, and he was notorious for responding when the pressure was on. Inducted in 1996.

BILL TERRY

New York Giants first baseman William Harold Terry was the last National League player to hit .400. He didn't join the Giants until he was 26, in 1923. It was 1927 before he established himself as the regular first baseman, whereupon he turned in six consecutive seasons of more than 100 runs and 100 RBI.

Terry became Giants manager in 1932 and led his team to a World Series victory as player-manager in 1933 and more pennants in 1936 and 1937. Terry had his greatest year in 1930. He batted .401 with a National League-record 254 hits, and tallied 77 extra-base hits, 139 runs, and 129 RBI. Terry was a standout with the glove as well, generally considered the best first

baseman of his day. He led the league in fielding average twice, assists and putouts five times each, and total chances per game nine times. Inducted in 1954.

MAJOR LEAGUE TOTALS			
BA	H	HR	RBI
.341	2,193	154	1,078

TED LYONS

Theodore Amar Lyons pitched 21 seasons with the Chicago White Sox, going 260-230 for a .531 winning percentage. In those years, without Lyons pitching, the White Sox compiled a .447 winning percentage. After a 1931 injury eight years into his career, he resurrected a knuckleball and pitched for 13 more seasons. Ted is the only Hall of Fame pitcher to serve 21 years with the same team without ever playing on a pennant winner. Inducted in 1955.

MAJOR LEAGUE TOTALS			
W	L	ERA	K
260	230	3.67	1,073

HEINIE MANUSH

Henry Emmett Manush was a pull hitter at the outset of his career, but by the time he reached the majors, he had already shortened his swing to punch the ball. Manush's adjustment was unusual, especially since he weighed around 200 pounds.

Manush claimed his production at bat benefited greatly from his long hours with his manager, Ty Cobb. He hit .330 in his 17-year career. Inducted in 1964.

MAJOR LEAGUE TOTALS			
BA	H	HR	RBI
.330	2,524	110	1,183

HACK WILSON

Never has anyone else in baseball looked quite like Lewis Robert Wilson. Only 5′6″ tall but weighing 200 pounds, Wilson had a huge barrel chest supported by tree-trunk-sized legs, resting on two tiny feet. He wore an 18-inch collar and size 6 shoes.

Originally a member of the Giants, Wilson slumped in his second season there and was claimed by the Cubs in 1925. During the next five years, Hack averaged 35 home runs, 141 RBI, and .331. He

won four home run titles in that span (1926-28 and 1930) and led the Cubs to the World Series in 1929 when he hit 39 homers and led the league with 159 RBI.

In 1930, Wilson rode the crest of an offensive wave that swept through baseball. He hit 56 home runs, the NL record, and drove in 190 runs, the major-league record. Hack was named *The Sporting News* MVP, but it was his last good year. Inducted in 1979.

MAJOR LEAGUE TOTALS			
BA	H	HR	RBI
.307	1,461	244	1,062

MARTIN DIHIGO

Since the Negro League teams obtained such slender profit margins, often teams carried only 14 to 18 players. The most valuable player to a team was usually the one

who could play several positions adequately. Martin Dihigo could pitch and play all the infield and outfield positions at an All-Star quality level. He is the only player enshrined in the Cuban, Mexican, and American halls of fame.

Cuban-born Dihigo also played in Puerto Rico, Mexico, and Venezuela. His Latin league pitching stats include an 18-2 record and an 0.90 ERA in 1938 and a 22-7 record and a 2.53 ERA in 1942. From the time he came to America in 1923 through 1936, he made only occasional forays to the pitching mound, having some success with his good fastball and control. He posted a .316 career batting average in the Negro Leagues. Inducted in 1977.

CHARLIE GEHRINGER

The possessor of an almost Sphinx-like demeanor, Charles Leonard Gehringer gave the same quietly outstanding performance day in and day out. His nickname was "The Mechanical Man." Mickey Cochrane, after managing Gehringer for two years in Detroit, said of him, "He says hello on opening day and goodbye on closing day, and in between he hits .350."

Signed by the Tigers in 1924 as a third baseman, Gehringer was soon moved to second base and became the club's regular there in 1926, holding the spot for 16 years. After a .277 rookie season, he batted over .300 every other season but one until he began to fade in 1941.

Gehringer's high watermark came in 1937 when he rapped .371 to win the American League batting crown. At age 34, he became the oldest first-time winner of a hitting title in history. Before 1937, Gehringer had also paced the junior loop on several occasions in runs, hits, doubles, triples, and stolen bases. Gehringer played in six All-Star Games and managed to hit a combined .500, cracking out 10 hits in 20 at bats. He displayed the same steady brilliance in his three World Series appearances with the Tigers. In 81 at bats, Gehringer hit .321—one point higher than his overall career batting average of .320. Inducted in 1949.

MAJOR LEAGUE TOTALS			
BA	H	HR	RBI
.320	2,839	184	1,427

AL SIMMONS

Al Simmons's career .334 batting average made mincemeat of critics who believed he would never be able to hit good pitching with his peculiar penchant for striding toward third base rather than toward the mound when he swung. This unorthodox batting style led to his tag, "Bucketfoot Al."

Born Aloysius Szymanski in a Polish section of Milwaukee, Simmons never wanted to be anything but a baseball player. In 1924, his rookie year with the A's, Simmons batted .308 and knocked home 102 runs. The following year, he collected a league-leading 253 hits and hiked his average to .387. He became the first player in AL history to drive in 100 or more runs in each of his first two seasons. Not only an outstanding hitter, Simmons was also an able outfielder with a strong throwing arm.

When the A's copped their first of three consecutive pennants in 1929, Simmons enjoyed the first of five straight seasons in which he got 200 or more hits, at the time an American League record. The following year, he won his first of two consecutive batting crowns and was generally regarded as the American League's most valuable player. Inducted in 1953.

MAJOR LEAGUE TOTALS			
BA	H	HR	RBI
.334	2,927	307	1,827

RED RUFFING

On May 6, 1930, Charles Herbert Ruffing had a 39-96 career win-loss record. But over the next 15 seasons, he won 231 games and posted a .651 winning percentage. More than any other pitcher in history, Ruffing proved what can happen when a good hurler on a poor team is traded to a contender.

In 1925, Ruffing found himself with the Red Sox, the worst club in the majors. The team had so little punch that pitcher Red was often

the best hitter in the lineup. Things changed after he was traded in May 1930 to the Yankees. Two years later, Ruffing bagged 18 victories as the Yankees copped their first flag under Joe McCarthy.

Before Red was done, he pitched on seven pennant winners in New York and had a 7-2 record in World Series play. Four times a 20-game winner, Ruffing was also the Yankees' chief right-handed pinch hitter for several seasons. Inducted in 1967.

MAJOR LEAGUE TOTALS			
W	L	ERA	K
273	225	3.80	1,987

EARLE COMBS

A great trivia question: Who had the most hits on the 1927 Yankees? The answer, surprisingly, is center fielder Earle Bryan Combs. Earle hit .356, collected 231 hits, scored 137 runs, and led the league in triples with 23.

Combs's average of .342 in 1925 is one of the highest in history for a rookie. Since he walked a fair amount and almost never struck out, Combs led off for the Yanks, scoring more than 100 runs in eight straight seasons. Although he didn't have a home run stroke, Combs led the league in triples three times (1927, 1928, and 1930), once hitting three in a single game.

Not having the strongest arm in the league, Combs's greatest asset was his speed as a fly hawk. He led

AL outfielders in putouts several years. Inducted in 1970.

MAJOR LEAGUE TOTALS			
BA	H	HR	RBI
.325	1,866	58	632

CHICK HAFEY

The frail, bespectacled Charles James "Chick" Hafey played more than 100 games in a season just seven times with only 1,466 hits and 833 RBI lifetime. Rogers Hornsby, however, called Hafey the greatest right-handed hitter he ever saw. In 1931, Chick won the NL batting title in the closest three-way batting race in history. Hafey checked in at .3489, Bill Terry of the Giants was at .3486, and Chick's St. Louis teammate Jim Bottomley batted .3482. Inducted in 1971.

MAJOR LEAGUE TOTALS			
BA	H	HR	RBI
.317	1,466	164	833

FRED LINDSTROM

Late in the 1924 season, 18-year-old Frederick Charles Lindstrom was forced to play third base for the Giants to replace an injured Heinie Groh. In that year's World Series, Lindstrom had a dubious debut when two balls bounced over his head in the final innings of Game 7. His team lost. However, Lindstrom built on that disappointment, eking

out a fine career with a solid glove and good bat. Inducted in 1976.

MAJOR LEAGUE TOTALS			
BA	H	HR	RBI
.311	1,747	103	779

BUCKY HARRIS

Bucky Harris earned his fame early as "The Boy Manager" of the Washington Senators and earned his Cooperstown credentials as one of the longest-running management acts in history, winning 2,157 games and managing five teams in eight stops during his 29-year career.

Stanley Raymond Harris was installed as the Senators manager in 1924, and with young star Goose Goslin and veteran Walter Johnson, the Senators pulled away from the Yankees with a great stretch drive.

As a manager, Harris was a hard man. He had only one taste of success after his first years in Washing-

ton. In 1947, he took over the Yankees and promptly won his second World Series. When the team finished third in 1948, Harris was sacked. He managed for seven more years in Washington and Detroit, never finishing higher than fifth. Inducted in 1975.

MAJOR LEAGUE TOTALS		
W	L	PCT
2,157	2,218	.493

LEFTY GROVE

Generally acknowledged as the greatest left-handed pitcher ever, Robert Moses Grove may well be the greatest pitcher, period. Along with the highest career winning percentage among pitchers with 300 or more victories, Grove also compiled a 112-39 record in the minors, giving him a combined percentage of .696, far and away the highest of any pitcher in organized baseball history.

Grove spent four and one-half years trapped in the minors because International League teams could retain their stars as long as they wished. Finally, after the 1924 season, Connie Mack bought Grove for $100,000 plus an extra $600 to make the price higher than what the Yankees paid for Babe Ruth.

Although not an instant star, Lefty topped the AL in wins four times, winning percentage five times, strikeouts seven times (in a row), and ERA nine times.

In 1930, he won 28 of 33 decisions and led the AL in winning percentage, ERA, and strikeouts. Incredibly, his 1931 season was better. That year, Grove had a 31-4 mark and an .886 winning percentage, the highest in history by a 30-game winner. The real topper, though, was his 2.06 ERA—2.32 runs per game below the league average. For his scorching performance, Grove received the first MVP Award given to an AL player by the Baseball Writers' Association of America. Inducted in 1947.

MAJOR LEAGUE TOTALS			
W	L	ERA	K
300	141	3.06	2,266

MICKEY COCHRANE

As a minor-league catcher, Gordon Stanley Cochrane caught the eye of Connie Mack. So certain was Mack of Cochrane's future greatness that he took over Portland in the Pacific Coast League to give Cochrane a place to hone his skills without danger of the A's losing him.

Joining the Mackmen in 1925, Cochrane caught a rookie-record 134 games while hitting .331. Cochrane laid claim throughout his career to being the best-hitting catcher in baseball. His .320 batting average and .419 on-base percentage are both career records for a catcher, and his .478 slugging average is an AL record. Cochrane also had an exceptional batting eye—he walked four times as often as he struck out.

Cochrane played on five pennant winners, three in Philadelphia and two more after he was traded to Detroit after the 1933 season. As player-manager, he won flags in 1934 and 1935, his first two seasons at the Detroit helm. After a 1937 beaning, Mickey hovered near death for more than a week before recovering. Cochrane was eager to get back into action, but Detroit owner Walter Briggs forbade it, especially since doctors had warned that a second beaning could prove fatal. Through as a player, Cochrane

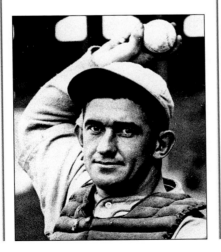

managed the Tigers another one-plus seasons. Inducted in 1947.

MAJOR LEAGUE TOTALS			
BA	H	HR	RBI
.320	1,652	119	832

MEL OTT

Melvin Thomas Ott stood out even in an era of great sluggers—for his youth, his stance, and his consistent performance for nearly two decades.

After signing Ott, John McGraw refused to send him to the minors for seasoning. McGraw feared that a farm skipper would alter Ott's unusual stance, thereby "ruining" him. Under McGraw's wing, Ott emerged as a star. Ott's stance was one of the oddest in baseball. He lifted his front foot before swinging, and he held his hands low, almost below his belt. The result was a level swing with terrific power, proved in 1929, his first season as a regular, when he hit 42 home runs with 151 RBI. He led the league with 113 walks, a sign of the discipline that led to a lifetime on-base average of .414. His youthful appearance and size (he was a compact 5'7", 160 pounds) reinforced the impression of youth that stayed with him throughout his career.

Ott was a fine outfielder with perhaps the best arm of his day. Though he was not slow, he did have some leg problems, but he managed to score 1,859 runs, one of history's highest totals. Ott benefited greatly from his home park, hitting "only" 187 road homers. Inducted in 1951.

MAJOR LEAGUE TOTALS			
BA	H	HR	RBI
.304	2,876	511	1,860

JIMMIE FOXX

In an era of big hitters, James Emory Foxx won four home run titles and two batting titles. He was the first ALer to win consecutive MVP Awards and the first man to win the award three times.

Both the Yankees and A's were interested in the young Foxx, but Frank "Home Run" Baker steered Foxx to the A's as a favor to Connie Mack. By the time Foxx became the regular first baseman in 1929, the A's were a powerhouse. "Double X," with Al Simmons and Lefty Grove, was the heart of Mack's last great team. Foxx appeared in three consecutive World Series from 1929 to 31. He belted an even 100 homers those three years and knocked in 394 runs. Foxx won consecutive MVP Awards in 1932 and 1933. He earned the Triple Crown in 1933 with 48 homers, 163 RBI, and a .356 average. The A's won two titles before bowing to St. Louis in seven games in 1931. That was Foxx's postseason swan song—he hit .344 and slugged .609 in 18 Series games.

At the time of his retirement, only Ruth had more home runs, and Foxx had hit more homers than anyone in the 1930s. He had three

seasons with slugging averages of over .700. Inducted in 1951.

MAJOR LEAGUE TOTALS			
BA	H	HR	RBI
.325	2,646	534	1,922

JOE CRONIN

In 1926, at age 20, Joseph Edward Cronin sat on the bench in Pittsburgh. In 1959, he became AL president. In between, he turned in a Hall of Fame career as one of the best hitting shortstops in history.

After two seasons as a Pirate, Cronin landed in Washington in 1928. In 1930, he won *The Sporting News* Most Valuable Player Award when he hit .346 with 127 runs and 126 RBI. Joe reached the 100-RBI mark in eight seasons, remarkable for a shortstop with his fielding ability. Cronin compiled a lifetime .301 batting average and was a spectacular doubles hitter, socking 51 in 1938 and 515 in his career. He was named the outstanding major-league shortstop by *The Sporting News* seven times.

Cronin was active in an era when player-managers were common, and he served a long term in that role in Washington and Boston. His maiden voyage as a manager (1933) produced a pennant. Cronin had many doubts about his double duty and tried to resign after his first season. He didn't finish first again until 1946, when he stepped down as a player, and brought Boston its first pennant since 1918.

In 1959, Cronin was elected president of the American League, the first former player so honored, remaining in the office until 1973. Inducted in 1956.

MAJOR LEAGUE TOTALS			
BA	H	HR	RBI
.301	2,285	170	1,424

JOE McCARTHY

Joe McCarthy's .615 managerial career winning percentage and his .698 World Series winning percentage are both the best of all time.

The Cubs signed Joseph Vincent McCarthy to manage after he sported six good seasons as player-manager with Louisville. McCarthy's first action with the Cubs was cutting Grover Alexander, establishing a reputation as a disciplinarian. But "Marse Joe" was very much a man behind the scenes and was remarkable for his low profile, despite the great success of his teams. McCarthy improved the Cubs each year, and the acquisition of Rogers Hornsby in 1929 provided the final ingredient to win the pennant. McCarthy then assumed control of the Yankees, skipperless after the death of Miller Huggins.

Babe Ruth wanted the Yankee manager job very badly, and it is a tribute to McCarthy's ability that he was able to deflect the Babe's resentment. The Yankees finished second in 1931, but in 1932 the Yanks beat McCarthy's old Chicago team in the World Series. In 1936 Joe DiMaggio joined the team, and the Yankees won four straight Series, winning 16 games while losing just three. In 1941, they won it all again. McCarthy brought them to the Series again in 1942 and 1943, winning his final championship in 1943. Inducted in 1957.

MAJOR LEAGUE TOTALS		
W	L	PCT
2,125	1,333	.615

PAUL WANER

Because at 5'9", 150 pounds, Paul Waner was bulkier than his brother Lloyd, he was called "Big Poison" and

Lloyd "Little Poison." The nicknames were Brooklynese for "person."

After pacing the Pacific Coast League in 1925 with a .401 batting average and 75 doubles, Paul Glee Waner was sold to Pittsburgh along with Hal Rhyne for $100,000 and three players, the largest sum ever paid for a minor-leaguer to that time.

Waner demonstrated his value immediately. In 1926, his rookie season, he hit .336, higher than any other NL regular, but Reds catcher Bubbles Hargrave, who had only 326 at bats, won the bat crown. When Lloyd joined Paul on the Bucs, the two combined to amass a sibling-record 460 hits in 1927 and help bring Pittsburgh the pennant. That year, Paul led the NL with a .380 average, 237 hits, 18 triples, and 131 RBI, winning the MVP Award.

Waner won three hitting titles and led the NL—at one time or another—in every major batting department except home runs and walks. En route to totaling 3,152 career hits, he set an NL record with 200 or more hits in a season on eight separate occasions. Inducted in 1952.

MAJOR LEAGUE TOTALS			
BA	H	HR	RBI
.333	3,152	113	1,309

LLOYD WANER

Lloyd James Waner was one of the smallest men to achieve star status. At 5'9" and just 135 pounds when he came up, he was even smaller

than his brother Paul. Lloyd played center field in the Pirates outfield alongside Paul for 14 campaigns. In his first three seasons, he hit .355, .335, and .353, collected more than 200 hits, and scored 120-plus runs each year. Inducted in 1967.

MAJOR LEAGUE TOTALS			
BA	H	HR	RBI
.316	2,459	27	598

TONY LAZZERI

Anthony Michael Lazzeri was a hard-hitting second baseman on the great Yankee teams of the 1920s. He received his nickname, "Poosh 'Em Up," for his habit of getting clutch hits with men on base.

In the Pacific Coast League, Lazzeri was the first player in history to belt 60 homers in a season. In 1926, Yankee manager Miller Huggins replaced shortstop Pee Wee Wanninger and second baseman Joe Dugan with Mark Koenig and Lazzeri. That move helped the Yanks score 847 runs in 1926 (Lazzeri had 114 RBI, second in the loop). Lazzeri had more than 100 RBI in seven seasons from 1926 to 1937 as the Yankee second sacker. He reached .300 in five seasons. Inducted in 1991.

MAJOR LEAGUE TOTALS			
BA	H	HR	RBI
.292	1,840	178	1,191

CARL HUBBELL

Carl Owen Hubbell was a winner. He had to be to earn the nickname "The Meal Ticket." In his 16 years with John McGraw's Giants, Hubbell won 253 games and lost 154, while posting a remarkable 2.98 earned run average.

When Tiger manager Ty Cobb refused to let Hubbell use his devastating screwball, Hubbell lost all confidence and was soon released. Discovered by a Giant scout, he tossed the league's only no-hitter in 1929, but his big years didn't begin until 1933, whereupon he registered five straight 20-plus victory seasons. In 1933, King Carl pitched a record 18-inning shutout, won two games in the World Series, pitched 20 Series innings without allowing an earned run (including a Series-record 11-inning whitewash), and was chosen the league's Most Valuable Player.

The following season, he had his most famous moment. In the All-Star Game in 1934, Hubbell fanned Babe Ruth, Lou Gehrig, Jimmie

Foxx, Al Simmons, and Joe Cronin in succession, electrifying the fans.

Hubbell won the MVP Award again in 1936 when he turned in one of the best pitching records in history at 26-6. Hubbell finished 1936 with 16 straight wins and won his first eight in 1937, for a 24-game winning streak. Inducted in 1947.

MAJOR LEAGUE TOTALS			
W	L	ERA	K
253	154	2.98	1,677

BILL DICKEY

Until Yogi Berra came along, William Malcolm Dickey was known not only as the greatest Yankee catcher but also as one of the greatest catchers of all time. He joined the Yankees late in the 1928 season. In 1929, his first full season, he batted .324. He was Lou Gehrig's roommate, and they were a matched set—quiet and consistent. Dickey topped the .300 mark 10 times. His mark of .362 in 1936 was a record for backstoppers. From 1936 to 1939, the left-handed Dickey popped 20-plus homers a year and drove in 100-plus runs.

A hard worker and a fierce competitor, Dickey handled Yankee pitching staffs on eight World Series teams, winning seven titles. His 17-year career spanned the era from Ruth to DiMaggio. Dickey caught 100 or more games for 13 consecutive seasons—a record that stood until Johnny Bench. At the time of Dickey's retirement, he

held the records for putouts and fielding average. After serving in World War II, he returned but played in only 54 more games. When the Yankees were working with a kid named Berra, Dickey was called in to show the youngster the ropes. Inducted in 1954.

MAJOR LEAGUE TOTALS			
BA	H	HR	RBI
.313	1,969	202	1,209

CHUCK KLEIN

In 1928, Charles Herbert Klein was purchased by the Phillies and immediately put into Philadelphia livery. In his rookie season, Klein tattooed an eye-opening 91 hits in just 64 games and batted .360. As a sophomore, Klein rapped .356 and set an NL record with 43 home runs. In 1930, his third season, Klein scored 158 runs (an NL record that still stands) and bagged 59 doubles. In addition, he batted .386, pounded out 250 hits, and collected 170 RBI.

During each of the next three seasons, Klein topped the NL in home runs and slugging average. His apex came in 1933 when he won the Triple Crown. Inducted in 1980.

MAJOR LEAGUE TOTALS			
BA	H	HR	RBI
.320	2,076	300	1,201

Chapter Four

HOME FRONT

America's Pastime at War

Baseball opened the 1940s with one eye on the growing conflict in Europe and another on its new legion of stars. Cleveland's Bob Feller began the decade with an Opening Day no-hitter. Shortly thereafter, however, many of the game's top stars donned military uniforms. An Army-Navy exhibition game played in Cleveland in mid-1942 drew 62,094 fans, because Feller was pitching for Mickey Cochrane's Great Lakes Naval Training team.

In January 1942, President Franklin D. Roosevelt asked commissioner Kenesaw Mountain Landis not to suspend play. "I honestly feel it would be best for the country to keep baseball going," the President wrote. The green-light letter did not save most major-leaguers from military service, but it did create major league jobs for 200 men who had been classified 4-F. Things got so desperate that the Cardinals advertised for players in 1943; other clubs followed suit. Within four years of Pearl Harbor, the armed forces had taken all but 400 of the 5,800 men in pro baseball at the time of the attack.

In 1946, baseball picked up where it had paused. Feller won 26 games, Ted Williams batted .342, and Stan Musial led the NL in six offensive categories. The minor leagues had also recovered, after many suspended operations during the war. The International League had a new batting champion: Jackie Robinson of the Montreal Royals.

A hot start in 1939 got Joe DiMaggio the cover of Life magazine. DiMaggio hit .381 that season to gain both his first AL batting crown and MVP Award. DiMaggio was the most popular ballplayer in the 1940s.

DIZZY DEAN

One of the most entertaining players in the history of baseball, Jay Hanna "Dizzy" Dean blazed across the baseball sky for five seasons. He was the last pitcher to win 30 games in one year until Denny McLain.

The league's Most Valuable Player in 1934, Dean then finished second in 1935 and 1936.

After winning 26 games in 1931 at Triple-A Houston, Dean was called up to the Cards to stay for the 1932 season. Dizzy won 18 games and led the NL in shutouts,

innings pitched, and strikeouts—the first of four consecutive strikeout titles he would earn.

Despite his flaky image, Dizzy was far from dumb and was, in fact, a shrewd negotiator. He staged a holdout during the 1934 season for his brother Paul, whom Dizzy felt

was underpaid. Despite missing some starts during the holdout, the elder Dean went 30-7, and rookie Paul was 19-11.

The Dean brothers won four World Series games in 1934 as the Cards beat the Tigers. During the 1937 All-Star Game, a line drive off the bat of Earl Averill broke Dizzy's toe. He tried to come back too soon, which altered his motion and, as a result, injured his right arm. He never fully recovered and never again won more than eight games in a season. Dean became a popular broadcaster with a unique gift for memorable malapropisms. Inducted in 1953.

MAJOR LEAGUE TOTALS			
W	L	ERA	K
150	83	3.02	1,163

HANK GREENBERG

Of the many players who lost playing time and had their career totals diminished by World War II, Henry Benjamin Greenberg may have lost

the most. He was active for only nine and one-half seasons, serving in the Army for four and one-half years; still, he was able to produce Hall of Fame numbers.

In 1934, Greenberg led the league with 63 doubles and drove in 139 runs. In 1935, the Tigers won a world championship and Hank won his first MVP Award, leading the league with 36 homers and 170 RBI. For the next four years, the Tigers vainly chased the Yankees before sinking to the second division. Greenberg's 183 RBI in 1937 is the third highest total in history, and his career rate of .92 RBI per game is matched only by Gehrig in this century. Greenberg challenged Babe Ruth's single-season home run record by clubbing 58 in 1938.

In 1940, Hammerin' Hank led the Tigers to a pennant and grabbed his second MVP Award as he led the league in doubles, homers, and, of course, RBI. He returned from the war to lead the Tigers to the world championship

in 1945, cracking a grand slam on September 30 to clinch the pennant. In 1946, Greenberg led the league in home runs and RBI, but it was to be his last good season. Inducted in 1956.

MAJOR LEAGUE TOTALS			
BA	H	HR	RBI
.313	1,628	331	1,276

EARL AVERILL

Howard Earl Averill was the first player in American League history to homer in his first major-league at bat. He went on to hit .332 for the Indians and compile 198 hits and 96 RBI in his rookie year of 1929. In addition, his 18 home runs established a Cleveland record to that point. For more than a decade, Averill continued his onslaught on American League pitchers. Inducted in 1975.

MAJOR LEAGUE TOTALS			
BA	H	HR	RBI
.318	2,019	238	1,164

LEFTY GOMEZ

Vernon Louis "Lefty" Gomez knew the value of playing for the powerhouse Yankees (he claimed the secret of his success was "clean living and a fast outfield"), but he was capable of smothering teams on his own with his wicked fastball and a fine curve. Although plagued by

arm ailments throughout his career, Gomez changed his style as he got older, perfecting a baffling slow curveball. He compiled a career 189-102 win-loss record.

The top winner on the Yanks in six of his 10 full seasons with them, Gomez also twice led the league in wins and ERA. In 1934 he was 26-5, leading the league in ERA, strikeouts, shutouts, and complete games. In 1932, when the Yankees finally unseated the Athletics, Gomez won 24 games in a spectacular clutch performance.

Gomez has the greatest World Series record in history, winning six games without a loss and winning five world championship rings. Inducted in 1972.

Major League Totals			
W	L	ERA	K
189	102	3.34	1,468

Josh Gibson

Possibly the best known of the Negro League sluggers, Joshua

Gibson rattled tape-measure home runs off the seats at a rate that could not be ignored. When he was barely in his 20s, this member of the Homestead Grays was hitting around 70 home runs a year. He was lured to the Pittsburgh Crawfords in 1932, where he caught Satchel Paige for five years.

Gibson reached distances in major-league parks undreamed of by the white players who played in them regularly. He is credited with hitting a ball out of Yankee Stadium, and his longest hits are variously estimated between 575 and 700 feet. His career total is uncertain, but even the lowest estimates put him ahead of Hank Aaron, with 800 to 950 career homers. Gibson's lifetime average is the highest in Negro League baseball: .379 or .440 depending on the source. Against major-league pitching in 16 exhibition games, he hit .424 with five homers.

Gibson returned to the Grays in 1937 but began to experience severe headaches and drink more

than was his habit, partly in a search for relief from what was finally diagnosed as a brain tumor. He died in 1947, the year Jackie Robinson joined the Brooklyn Dodgers. Inducted in 1972.

Arky Vaughan

A nine-time All-Star, Joseph Floyd "Arky" Vaughan was one of the greatest offensive shortstops in baseball history. He led the NL three times in walks, triples, runs, and on-base percentage. He also led the loop in putouts and assists three times, proving he was no slouch with the glove.

Vaughan retired with a .318 career batting average, the second highest in history by a shortstop. Because he broke in with Pittsburgh, Arky invited immediate comparison with Honus Wagner, a comparison he and every other shortstop could not but suffer from the making. Although never Wagner's equal in the field, Arky gave him a close run offensively. Vaughan's .385 season in 1935 not only achieved the National League batting crown but also set a then-20th-century loop record for the highest average by a shortstop. A year later, he garnered 118 walks to carve out another senior-circuit record for shortstops.

In the 1941 All-Star Game at Briggs Stadium in Detroit, Vaughan became the first player to hit two home runs in a midsummer classic when he rapped a two-run dinger in the seventh inning and then repeated his feat in the eighth. Inducted in 1985.

MAJOR LEAGUE TOTALS			
BA	H	HR	RBI
.318	2,103	96	926

LUKE APPLING

Lucius Benjamin Appling was a batsman second to none, hitting over .300 16 times in his 20-year career. He had outstanding command of the strike zone, once fouling off over a dozen pitches in a single at bat.

He became the White Sox full-time shortstop in 1933 and won the first of his two batting titles in 1936 when he hit .388, his career high. Appling hit .317 in 1937, and in 1938, with a broken leg, still managed to hit over .300. He won another batting title in 1943 with a .328 average, but in 1944 he was off to war. When he returned, Appling hit over .300 each year from 1946 to 1949. His persistent knee and

back problems earned him the nickname "Old Aches and Pains."

When Luke retired he left behind all-time records for major-league shortstops in games and double plays, as well as American League records for putouts, assists, and total chances. The records lasted 23 years until fellow Soxer Luis Aparicio broke them. Appling awakened memories of his greatness when he hit a home run in the first Crackerjack Old-Timer's Game in Washington, D.C., in 1985, when he was 78 years old. Luke never got the chance to play in a World Series, but he sustained a remarkable level of performance for an astounding length of time. Inducted in 1964.

MAJOR LEAGUE TOTALS			
BA	H	HR	RBI
.310	2,749	45	1,116

BILLY HERMAN

Until Rod Carew retired in 1985, William Jennings Bryan Herman was the last player to appear in 1,000 or more games at second base and retire with a career batting average above .300. During his 15 major-league seasons, he participated in 10 All-Star Games and played on four pennant winners.

In his first full big-league campaign with the Cubs, Herman tied for the National League lead in games played with 154, batted .314, and collected 206 hits. In 1935, he collected 57 doubles, a record for

National League second basemen. Herman topped NL second basemen in putouts a record seven times and ranked as the best all-around keystone sacker in the senior loop for nearly a decade.

Traded to the Dodgers in 1941, Herman sparked Brooklyn to their first flag in 21 years. Herman and shortstop Pee Wee Reese gave Brooklyn one of the top keystone combinations in the game. Inducted in 1975.

MAJOR LEAGUE TOTALS			
BA	H	HR	RBI
.304	2,345	47	839

BILL MCKECHNIE

William Boyd McKechnie had a remarkable record as a manager, even though he never obtained the reins of a great team. In 1935, McKechnie had the misfortune to be at the helm of the worst team in modern National League history, the 38-115 Boston Braves. But he won pennants with three different teams—the Pirates, Cardinals, and Reds—the first manager to accomplish this feat. Inducted in 1962.

MAJOR LEAGUE TOTALS		
W	L	PCT
1,896	1,723	.524

ERNIE LOMBARDI

Ernesto Natali Lombardi retired with the fourth highest batting average in history among catchers who appeared in more than 1,000 games. Those who saw him play insist his .306 mark would have been 50 points higher if he had even average speed. Lombardi was so slow afoot that infielders customarily played him back on the outfield grass, thus cutting off many screeching line drives that otherwise would have been hits.

As a Red from 1934 to 1937, Lombardi hit .305, .343, .333, and .334, respectively, with about 60 RBI a season. In 1938, he became the first receiver in major-league

history to win an undisputed batting crown when he hit .342 for the Reds in 489 at bats. With Lombardi behind the plate and a pitching tandem of Paul Derringer and Bucky Walters, in 1939 the Reds grabbed their first pennant since 1919 and repeated in 1940. Inducted in 1986.

MAJOR LEAGUE TOTALS			
BA	H	HR	RBI
.306	1,792	190	990

JOE MEDWICK

Never one to back off from an altercation, Joseph Michael Medwick was the principal in a famous World Series incident. In 1934's seventh game between the Tigers and Medwick's Cardinals, Medwick's hard slide into third sacker Marv Owen led the partisan Detroit fans to pelt him with garbage when he headed to his position in left field at the bottom of the inning. Commissioner Landis ordered Medwick removed from the game for his own safety.

Medwick was deemed ready to replace defending batting champ Chick Hafey in the St. Louis lineup late in 1932. Joe hit .300 every year from 1933 to 1942, topping 100 RBI from 1934 to 1939. In 1936, he led the National League in hits and RBI and set a new loop record with 64 doubles. The following year, Medwick became the last player in National League history to win a Triple Crown. Inducted in 1968.

MAJOR LEAGUE TOTALS			
BA	H	HR	RBI
.324	2,471	205	1,383

RAY DANDRIDGE

One of the greatest fielding third basemen in baseball history, Ray Dandridge was also a high average hitter who, at age 36, batted .362 in the American Association.

Raymond Dandridge joined the barnstorming Detroit Stars in 1933, where his coach encouraged him to shift to a heavy bat to make contact. Ray compiled a .355 lifetime average in the Negro Leagues and hit .347 against white major-leaguers. Defensively, Dandridge had terrific reflexes, with a glove often compared with Brooks Robinson's.

Signed by the Minneapolis Millers of the American Association in 1949, Dandridge narrowly missed the batting title with a .362 average and was voted the loop's Rookie of the Year. In 1950, he hit .311 and won the MVP Award. He *(continued on page 59)*

JOE DiMAGGIO

I f Joseph Paul DiMaggio wasn't the greatest all-around player in baseball history, he almost certainly was the most majestic.

In his 1936 rookie season, DiMaggio joined with Lou Gehrig to power the Yankees to the first of four consecutive world championships. Although severely hampered by Yankee Stadium's cavernous left field, "The Yankee Clipper" twice led the league in home runs and twice in slugging. He hit only 148 of his 361 lifetime home runs at home.

DiMaggio was an outstanding and beautiful defensive outfielder. He played center with grace and threw the ball with terrific power. He led the league in assists with 22 his rookie year, and had 21 and then 20 before the league stopped running on him.

Joltin' Joe won his first Most Valuable Player Award in 1939, when he had his career-best .381 batting average. When he won his second MVP in 1941, he had 76 walks and only 13 strikeouts. He also hit in a record 56 consecutive games, a feat some observers consider his greatest: No other player has ever hit in more than 44 straight. DiMaggio almost never struck out—his high was 39, his rookie year; he actually came close to having more lifetime homers than Ks, with 369 strikeouts to his 361 round-trippers.

If Yankee Stadium depressed his career totals, World War II was even more of a factor as Joe lost three seasons. He won his third MVP Award and the Yankees won another championship in 1947 (it was Joe who hit the drive that made Al Gionfriddo famous), but a heel injury slowed Joe in 1948, and he couldn't return to the lineup until June 1949. His return was memorable: He had four homers and nine RBI in a doubleheader. Another world championship followed, the first of five straight for the Yanks, but DiMaggio would stick around for only three of them. Injuries and the grind of the road drove Joe into retirement after the 1951 season. He was succeeded in center by Mickey Mantle.

DiMaggio was a joy to watch, and he loved to play the game. With the passing of time, Joe's legend continued to grow. Ernest Hemingway mentions Joe in *The Old Man and the Sea*, and musicians from Les Brown to Paul Simon wrote songs about him. He was briefly married to another American icon, Marilyn Monroe. Inducted in 1955.

MAJOR LEAGUE TOTALS			
BA	H	HR	RBI
.325	2,214	361	1,537

DiMaggio accepts the AL MVP Award in 1948.

(continued from page 57)
also became mentor to teammate Willie Mays. But Dandridge was never called up, and he never forgave Giants owner Horace Stoneham. Inducted in 1987.

ED BARROW

Sportswriter, concessionaire, minor-league manager, owner, and league president, Edward Grant Barrow became the manager of the Boston Red Sox in 1917. The club promptly won the 1918 World Series.

After the 1920 season, Barrow was appointed business manager of the Yankees, a position he held for the next 27 years. More than any other man, Barrow was responsible for developing the Yankees into the greatest dynasty in professional sports history. Inducted in 1953.

BUCK LEONARD

Walter Fenner "Buck" Leonard, a left-handed power-hitting first baseman, often drew comparisons to Lou Gehrig. Buck was a key ingredient in the powerful Homestead Grays of the 1930s.

When Josh Gibson joined them in 1937, the Grays caught fire, winning nine consecutive flags. And when Gibson jumped to Mexico in 1940, Leonard carried the club, hitting .392 in 1941 to lead the Negro National League. He won another batting title when he was 41 years old, with a .395 average and a share of the league's home run title.

Leonard was paid fairly well for his services: The Grays were forced to match the salary he was offered to play in Mexico. Buck commanded more than $1,000 per month in 1942 and even more later. He stayed with the Grays his entire career, instead of jumping to other teams as other Negro League stars had done. Inducted in 1972.

LARRY MACPHAIL

Leland Stanford MacPhail bought the declining Columbus, Ohio, franchise in the American Association in 1930. In 1934, he became general manager of the nearly bankrupt Cincinnati Reds. He introduced night baseball and air travel to the major leagues, and he also built pennant winners in 1939 and 1940, although he had moved to the Dodgers before he could enjoy the fruits of his success. The highlights of MacPhail's tenure in Brooklyn include putting lights in Ebbets Field and bringing in Red Barber to broadcast Dodger games.

Larry solidified a reputation as a slick trader and a baseball power.

After serving in World War II, MacPhail became part-owner of the New York Yankees, with a 10-year contract to run the team. As president and general manager, he helped build what would become the most successful team in baseball history. Inducted in 1978.

LEON DAY

Leon Day was only average in stature, but his talent was so abundant that he was able to play three positions for several Negro League teams. Primarily a pitcher, and noted for his no-windup style, Day played second base or the outfield when he wasn't on the mound. Bedridden with diabetes and a heart condition when he was elected to the Hall, he said, "They could have done it when I could have enjoyed it more." Inducted in 1995.

BILL VEECK

William Veeck Jr. was not the first owner to realize that baseball is in the business of entertainment, but he did more than any other owner during his time to entertain the fan. The other owners belittled his promotions but eventually used his ideas.

He revived the Milwaukee franchise in the American Association with various gimmicks, then sold it in 1945, purchasing the Cleveland Indians in 1946. Soon the team was setting attendance records. Bill signed the first African American to play in the American League, Larry Doby. In 1948, Veeck signed Negro League legend Satchel Paige. As owner of the St. Louis Browns, he sent Eddie Gaedel, a 3'7", 65-pound entertainer, up to bat.

Bill owned the White Sox twice. After he sold the team for the second time, he was often seen across town in the bleachers of Wrigley Field, shirtless and holding a beer, among the people he loved the best, the fans. Inducted in 1991.

BOB FELLER

Robert William Andrew Feller was illegally signed by Cleveland in 1935 while still a 16-year-old high school student. The Indians could have lost the rights to Feller had commissioner Kenesaw Mountain Landis not feared a gargantuan bidding war among the other teams if Feller was made a free agent. Even as a teenager, Feller was renowned for the blazing fastball that would soon gain him the nickname "Rapid

Robert." His exhibition game debut at age 17 had people comparing him with Walter Johnson.

All did not come easy, though, for Feller. Batters learned quickly that although he was virtually unhittable, they could reach base by waiting for walks. In 1938, he fanned 18 Tigers to set a modern record, yet he lost the contest, partly due to walks. That year, Rapid Robert also set a new modern mark for bases on balls—208.

His control slowly improving, Feller paced the American League in wins during each of the next three seasons and then went into the Navy. Returning from the war, Feller had his finest season in 1946 when he won 26 games and logged 348 strikeouts. An arm injury in 1947 curtailed Bob's fastball thereafter, but he continued to be one of the game's top hurlers until 1955. He was the author of three career no-hitters and 12 one-hit games. Inducted in 1962.

MAJOR LEAGUE TOTALS			
W	L	ERA	K
266	162	3.25	2,581

BOBBY DOERR

Robert Pershing Doerr was a great hitting second baseman who drove in more than 100 runs six times as the Red Sox finished first or second in seven of his 14 seasons.

Right-handed-hitting Doerr took advantage of Fenway Park's peculiarities to hit for terrific

power. He led the league in slugging in 1944 with a career-high .528 mark, while batting .325. Although a teammate and good friend of scientific batsman Ted Williams, Doerr was primarily an intuitive guess hitter. With a .288 lifetime average, Doerr collected 2,042 hits, 223 home runs, and 1,247 RBI. In 1950, Doerr led the league in triples, hit 27 dingers, and drove home 120 runs.

A solid fielder, Doerr remains in the all-time top ten for putouts and assists for second basemen, even though many second sackers have enjoyed much longer careers than he did. In the 1948 near-pennant year, Doerr accepted 414 chances without an error—almost three errorless months. Inducted in 1986.

MAJOR LEAGUE TOTALS			
BA	H	HR	RBI
.288	2,042	223	1,247

JOHNNY MIZE

Hard-hitting first baseman John Robert Mize joined the Cards in

1936 and batted .329. He surpassed the .300 mark for the next eight years, peaking at .364 in 1937. In 1939, Johnny led the league in homers (28) and batting average (.349).

Traded to the New York Giants for the 1942 season, Mize led the NL with a .521 slugging percentage and 110 RBI. After three years in the Navy, he returned to top the NL twice in home runs, including 51 round-trippers in 1947—a mark that still stands for NL lefties—tying Ralph Kiner for the league's top spot. And Mize paced the loop in RBI (138) and runs scored (137).

Acquired by the Yankees in late 1949, he was a star in two World Series, and led the AL in pinch hits from 1951 to 1953. Mize is the only slugger in history to hit three home runs in a game six times. Inducted in 1981.

MAJOR LEAGUE TOTALS			
BA	H	HR	RBI
.312	2,011	359	1,337

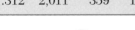

ENOS SLAUGHTER

For 19 years, Enos Bradsher Slaughter was the epitome of hustle, a quality that permeated all facets of his game.

Slaughter won the right-field job with the Cards in 1938 and was soon noted for his constant effort. He batted .320 in 1939, scoring 95 runs. He hit .306 in 1940 with 96 runs scored, and batted .311 in 1941.

A .300 lifetime hitter, "Country" topped the .300 mark 10 times. He collected 2,383 hits in 19 years. Had he not missed three years due to World War II, Slaughter would have been within striking distance of 3,000. He led the senior loop in hits in 1942 (188), in RBI in 1946 (130), in doubles in 1939 (52), and in triples twice, in 1942 and 1949. Slaughter also worked hard on his defense, overcoming a reputation for wildness by developing a strong and accurate throwing arm. Inducted in 1985.

MAJOR LEAGUE TOTALS			
BA	H	HR	RBI
.300	2,383	169	1,304

LOU BOUDREAU

Most analysts rate Louis Boudreau one of the best shortstops ever. In 1940, his initial year as a Cleveland regular, he hit .295 and drove in 101 runs. The next season, he topped the AL in doubles. In 1944, Lou copped the bat crown and seemed

headed for a repeat win the next season until a broken ankle sidelined him.

Before the 1942 campaign, although just 24, Lou was named Cleveland's manager, becoming the youngest pilot ever to open the season. Known as the "Boy Manager," Boudreau quickly showed he was mature beyond his years. A born leader, he demonstrated remarkable self-confidence and a willingness to experiment. He created the famous "Williams Shift" in 1946 to combat lefty pull-hitter Ted Williams, and changed strong-armed Bob Lemon from a third baseman to a pitcher. His Indians won the world championship in 1948, and Boudreau was the AL MVP, hitting .355 during the regular season and belting two homers in the playoff game. Inducted in 1970.

MAJOR LEAGUE TOTALS			
BA	H	HR	RBI
.295	1,779	68	789

BILL McGOWAN

Bill McGowan's career as an umpire began in 1925, and during his tenure he developed such a reputation for fairness, accuracy, and integrity that he earned the nickname "No. 1." McGowan was tough enough to work every inning of 2,541 consecutive games. He also worked eight World Series and four All-Star Games. Inducted in 1992.

RICK FERRELL

When Rick Ferrell retired, he had caught more games than any previous AL backstop, and he was one of the most respected receivers in baseball history, playing more than 18 seasons for three teams. He led the league in various defensive categories 11 times.

His brother, Wes, won 20 games six times, and they formed a battery for four years when they both played for Boston and Washington. Inducted in 1984.

MAJOR LEAGUE TOTALS			
BA	H	HR	RBI
.281	1,692	28	734

LEO DUROCHER

Everything in Leo Ernest Durocher's life seemed to take place on a grand scale. He played with Babe Ruth and managed both Jackie Robinson and Willie Mays. A member of the "Gashouse Gang" in 1934, he also helped create the 1951 "Miracle at Coogan's Bluff" for the Giants. He was suspended for fraternizing with gamblers, staged fierce arguments with umpires, and coined the phrase "Nice guys finish last," although his version was a little racier.

After a 17-year career as a big-league shortstop, he became the Dodgers manager in 1939; two years later he had them in the World Series, although not without famous and furious spats with equally volatile owner Larry MacPhail. After being fired for good by Brooklyn in 1948, Durocher went to the crosstown rival New York Giants. In eight years with the Giants, Durocher won two pennants and one World Series. He managed the Cubs and Astros in the 1960s and '70s. Inducted in 1994.

MAJOR LEAGUE TOTALS		
W	L	PCT
2,008	1,709	.540

HAL NEWHOUSER

Harold Newhouser spent 15 of 17 big-league seasons with his hometown Tigers. The erratic hurler was greatly helped by the arrival of Paul Richards as his catcher in 1943. Newhouser developed into the AL's premier war-time pitcher. His 29-9 record with a 2.22 ERA in 1944 earned him his first MVP Award. He recaptured the Award in '45, going 25-9 with a 1.81 ERA, and the Tigers won the World Series.

Newhouser paralyzed opponents with his fastball, curve, and change-up. With 152 victories under his belt by the time he was 27 years old, Newhouser seemed certain to challenge Eddie Plank's then-record for lefty wins, but shoulder pain brought him down after the 1948 season. Newhouser followed his 18 wins in 1949 with 15 in 1950, but he never reached double figures again. Inducted in 1992.

MAJOR LEAGUE TOTALS			
W	L	ERA	K
207	150	3.06	1,796

Chapter Five
EQUAL OPPORTUNITY

Robinson Erases the Line

A fter starring in four sports at UCLA and serving as an Army lieutenant, Jackie Robinson was selected by Branch Rickey of the Brooklyn Dodgers in 1946 to break baseball's color line. Rickey told Robinson that he required a talented player "with guts enough not to fight back."

Once the gifted but outspoken Robinson agreed, Rickey sent him to the Dodgers' top Triple-A farm club in Montreal for a year of physical and mental preparation. In 1947, when Robinson was placed on the Brooklyn roster, several teammates circulated a petition protesting his presence. Members of the Phillies and Cardinals undertook to strike—until commissioner Happy Chandler threatened lifetime suspensions for anyone who participated.

Though deluged with taunts from rival dugouts, Robinson kept his word and his cool. He not only survived the abuse but proved so talented a hitter, runner, and fielder that he was named Rookie of the Year in 1947. Two years later, he was the NL's Most Valuable Player. Robinson's arrival opened the door for others. Larry Doby of the Cleveland Indians became the American League's first black player later in 1947, and Satchel Paige, Roy Campanella, Don Newcombe, Monte Irvin, and Hank Thompson soon followed.

In 1953, the Braves changed the baseball map for the first time in 50 years by moving from Boston to Milwaukee. The Braves' immediate success convinced other clubs in two-team towns to seek greener pastures. The St. Louis Browns became the Baltimore Orioles in 1954, and the Philadelphia Athletics moved to Kansas City in '55.

Roy Campanella was featured on this Time *magazine cover. In 1953, he set a record with 41 home runs and 142 RBI generated by a player who served at no other position but catcher.*

SATCHEL PAIGE

Sometimes it seems Leroy Robert "Satchel" Paige was more a mythological being than a flesh-and-blood man. He was ageless, could do anything with a baseball, and few who faced him could help but acknowledge his greatness. He was the most popular baseball player in the Negro Leagues. After Jackie Robinson and Larry Doby integrated the major leagues, Paige was still baseball's biggest draw.

Paige gained fame when he joined the Pittsburgh Crawfords in the early 1930s. When he barnstormed around the country, fans would come to see his teams only when Paige pitched, so he pitched every day. He would promise to fan the first nine men he faced and often delivered on that promise. He proved he could pitch against the best in the major leagues. Paige was fantastically well paid for the time, earning close to $50,000 a year.

When a sore arm led to a demotion in 1939, Paige developed several off-speed pitches and hesitation deliveries that left hitters helpless. When his arm recovered the next season, he was a better pitcher than he had ever been.

Finally, in 1948 Bill Veeck signed Paige to a Cleveland contract. Paige went 6-1, pitching before packed houses, and the Indians won the pennant. Paige's last big-league appearance came in 1965 at age 59. He continued to pitch well in the minor leagues for years. Inducted in 1971.

MAJOR LEAGUE TOTALS			
W	L	ERA	K
28	31	3.29	288

CAL HUBBARD

At 265 pounds, umpire Robert Cal Hubbard backed down from no one. An All-American football play-er in 1926, he played pro ball for 10 years and was elected to both the College and Pro Football Halls of Fame.

His big-league umpiring career began the year his football career ended, 1936. Known for his uncanny knowledge of the rule book, he worked three All-Star Games and four World Series in his career. Inducted in 1976.

WILLIAM HARRIDGE

William Harridge was the American League president for 28 years, yet his is one of the least-recognized names on baseball's short list of administrators. He was a man behind the scenes. Harridge got his start in baseball as personal secretary to Ban Johnson, and he helped Johnson keep the growing American League together for 16 years. Harridge also worked for Johnson's successor and became AL president in 1931. Inducted in 1972.

GEORGE WEISS

George Weiss developed talent for the New York Yankees club that won nine pennants and eight World Series from 1947 to 1960. Hired in 1932 to mimic the success of Branch Rickey's Cardinals, Weiss came through.

His charges included Joe Gordon, Charlie Keller, Phil Rizzuto, and Yogi Berra. In 1949, then-GM Weiss hired Casey Stengel. Weiss snatched pennant insurance such as Johnny Mize and Enos Slaughter and stole Roger Maris from Kansas City. And his farm system produced Mickey Mantle and Whitey Ford. Inducted in 1971.

FORD FRICK

As president of the National League, Ford Christopher Frick used the power of his office to guarantee that Jackie Robinson would break the color line in 1947. Frick also furthered the idea behind the Baseball Hall of Fame in Cooperstown and administered baseball's expansion. A sportswriter and publicist, he was also Babe Ruth's ghostwriter. Frick served two seven-year terms as commissioner. Inducted in 1970.

CASEY STENGEL

Renowned for his unique misuse of the English language, Charles Dillon Stengel was as smart a field general and judge of talent as baseball ever produced.

(continued on page 66)

TED WILLIAMS

Theodore Samuel Williams once said he had a dream of walking down the street and having people point to him and say, "There goes Ted Williams, the greatest hitter who ever lived." Some baseball historians make that claim, with Babe Ruth his competition. But Williams holds the distinction of working harder than anyone at hitting.

After winning the American Association Triple Crown in 1938 with a .366 average, 43 homers, and 142 RBI, Williams made an immediate impact in Boston. He finished his rookie season in 1939 with a .327 average, 31 homers, and a league-leading 145 RBI. He led the AL with 134 runs scored while batting .344 in 1940. In 1941, Williams hit .406, the last man to hit over .400. Going into a doubleheader on the season's final day, he was at .39955. Manager Joe Cronin gave Ted the opportunity to sit down and

Williams wore a Red Sox uniform throughout his entire major-league career.

protect his average, which would have rounded up to .400, but Williams played both games and went 6-for-8. In 1942, Williams produced his first major-league Triple Crown, with a .356 average, 36 home runs, and 137 RBI, although he lost the MVP Award to Yankee Joe Gordon.

Williams spent three years as a pilot in World War II, returning in 1946 to lead Boston to his only pennant and winning his first MVP Award. "Teddy Ballgame" captured his second Triple Crown in 1947 (with a .343 batting average, 32 home runs, and 114 RBI) but was again denied the MVP Award, losing to Joe DiMaggio. Ted won the batting crown in 1948 (.369 average) and was again named MVP in 1949, hitting .343 with a league-leading 43 homers, 159 RBI, 150 runs, and 162 walks.

In 1952, at age 34, he was recalled for the Korean War, where he flew 39 missions, missing most of two more seasons. He failed to win batting titles in 1954 and 1955 because he fell short in at bats. He got two more batting crowns when he hit .388 (with 38 homers) in 1957 and .328 in 1958 at the ages of 39 and 40. When he hit a career-low .254 in 1959, he was urged to retire. Williams was too proud to leave with poor numbers and returned in 1960, hitting .316 with 29 home runs, including one in his last at bat.

Despite missing five years to military duty, Williams compiled astounding career numbers: the highest on-base average in history at .483; the second-highest slugging average at .634; the second-highest number of walks at 2,019. And he hit 521 home runs. Inducted in 1966.

MAJOR LEAGUE TOTALS			
BA	H	HR	RBI
.344	2,654	521	1,839

(continued from page 64)

After a 14-year playing career and several minor-league managing seasons, Stengel coached in Brooklyn for two seasons and got his first major-league managing stint in 1934 with the Dodgers. Stengel managed Brooklyn from 1934 to 1936. In 1938, the Boston Braves hired him, and he had no first-division finishes from 1938 to 1943. By 1944, Stengel was managing back in Triple-A.

In 1949, in a surprise move, the Yankees hired Stengel. His team had Yogi Berra and Joe DiMaggio, and Mickey Mantle and Whitey Ford were waiting in the wings. Together they put together five straight World Series wins. Stengel was largely responsible for the revival of platooning. In his 12 years with the Bombers, they won 10 pennants and seven World Series, success unmatched in professional ball. But the 1960 World Series loss cost Casey his job. He took over the expansion Mets in 1962 but lost 120 games, although Stengel took it with a smile. Stengel had a way with words that can't be imitated; the press dubbed it "Stengelese." In his baseball career, he saw the bottom and the top, and as he said, "There comes a time in every man's life and I've had plenty of them." Inducted in 1966.

MAJOR LEAGUE TOTALS		
W	L	PCT
1,905	1,842	.508

MONTE IRVIN

"Most of the black ballplayers thought Monte Irvin should have been the first black in the major leagues. Monte was our best young ballplayer at the time. He could do everything." So said Cool Papa Bell.

Monford Merrill Irvin was a star in the Negro Leagues. He was the acknowledged batting leader in 1940 and 1941. In Mexico in 1942, he hit .398 with power. The Giants picked up the 29-year-old Irvin from the defunct Newark Eagles in 1948. Irvin batted .299 with 15 homers for the Giants in 1950. In 1951, Monte hit .312 and led the league with 121 RBI. The Giants faced the Yankees in the World Series, and although they lost, Irvin hit .458. He called that season "The high point of my life." Inducted in 1973.

MAJOR LEAGUE TOTALS			
BA	H	HR	RBI
.293	731	99	443

PEE WEE REESE

Harold Henry "Pee Wee" Reese was the leader of the 1940s and '50s Brooklyn Dodgers. He was an outstanding shortstop and, despite his short stature, he stood so tall among his teammates that he was able to silence a team revolt against Jackie Robinson in 1947.

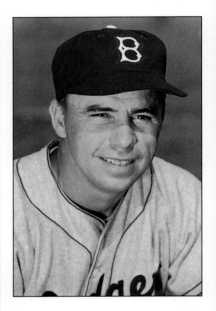

With a nickname from his marble-playing days, Pee Wee wasn't a great player immediately, but he became important to the Dodgers as a hitter, fielder, and leader. Reese spent three years in the Navy during World War II but returned to the Dodgers to become the old man of the Boys of Summer, the "Little Colonel" of the team that won six pennants in Reese's 12 postwar seasons. He was a complete player who, despite limited power, helped make the offense go and was an anchor on defense. His play won Reese top ten mention in

MVP voting eight times. Inducted in 1984.

MAJOR LEAGUE TOTALS			
BA	H	HR	RBI
.269	2,170	126	885

PHIL RIZZUTO

Philip Francis Rizzuto spent 13 years in the major leagues and, using spirit that went well beyond his physical size, went to nine World Series. His election to the Hall finally gave recognition to what baseball fans have long understood: Even on a team of power hitters and All-Star pitchers, someone must make the plays, move the runners along, and generally provide the chemistry that makes the whole thing work. "Scooter" did all of that.

One of the best bunters of his time, Rizzuto was named to five

All-Star Teams. In 1950, he batted .324 with 200 hits, 92 walks, and 125 runs scored, which earned him the Most Valuable Player Award. He batted .320 in the 1951 World Series.

After his playing career, Rizzuto settled into a long stint as the Yankees beloved radio announcer. Inducted in 1994.

MAJOR LEAGUE TOTALS			
BA	H	HR	RBI
.273	1,588	38	563

EARLY WYNN

Early Wynn had a rough go of it early in his career. He produced one good year with Washington—1943—when he went 18-12 with a 2.91 ERA. After nine frustrating years in Washington in which he compiled a 72-87 record, Wynn joined the Cleveland Indians in 1949 and changed the course of his career. In 1951, he won 20 games for the first time. He then won 23 in 1952, a league-leading 23 in 1954, and 20 in 1956. In 1954, Wynn led the league with 23 wins, his third 20-win season in four years. Wynn had eight winning records in the nine years he pitched in Cleveland.

Among the meanest head-hunters in the game, Wynn reportedly once said he would knock down his own mother if she dug in against him. His 1,544 strikeouts were the most in the 1950s. Inducted in 1972.

MAJOR LEAGUE TOTALS			
W	L	ERA	K
300	244	3.54	2,334

AL BARLICK

Along with Bill Summers, Albert Barlick holds the record for working the most All-Star Games—seven. In 1940, at age 26, Barlick joined the National League and was immediately recognizable due to his loud, flamboyant strike calls and "out" gestures even fans in the cheap seats couldn't miss. He was a hustling umpire who inspired respect among managers; they could never accuse him of not "bearing down." Inducted in 1989.

BOB LEMON

Robert Granville Lemon is the only 20th-century player in the Hall of Fame who began his major-league career as a hitter and subsequently

(continued on page 69)

Stan Musial

Stanley Frank Musial starred for the St. Louis Cardinals for 22 seasons and was the first National League player to win three Most Valuable Player Awards.

A good-hitting pitcher in the minors, Musial's career on the mound ended when he injured his left shoulder attempting a diving outfield catch. In 1942, the emerging Cardinal powerhouse won the first of three straight pennants as the rookie Musial hit .315. In 1943, he won his first MVP Award, leading the league with a .357 batting average, 220 base hits, 48 doubles, and 20 triples. He led the NL in hits and doubles again in 1944.

Musial had good home run power and terrific doubles power and, for his time, was a spectacular triples hitter. Terrifically fast—one of his nicknames was "The Donora Greyhound"—he was a fine fielder in left and later as a first baseman. Though he never led the league in homers, Musial won six slugging titles and in 1954 hit five round-trippers in a doubleheader. His unique corkscrew batting stance resulted in seven batting crowns. He posted a lifetime .416 on-base average, scoring at least 105 runs in 11 straight seasons.

Away in the Navy in 1945, Stan the Man came back in 1946 to win his second MVP Award as the Cards won another world championship. He led the league with a .365 batting average, 50 doubles, 20 triples, and 124 runs scored. Musial won his third Most Valuable Player trophy in 1948. He missed the Triple Crown by a single home run, hitting a career-high 39. He had a .376 average (the NL's highest since Bill Terry hit .401 in 1930), 230 base hits, 46 doubles, 18 triples, 131 RBI, and 135 runs scored, all of which led the NL. In addition to his three MVP Awards, Musial finished second four times.

A Cardinals jersey autographed by Stan the Man.

Stan won batting crowns from 1950 to 1952 (with averages of .346, .355, and .336, respectively), but the Cardinals could finish no better than third. Musial won his final batting title in 1957 at age 37, and the Redbirds finished second. Musial hit .330 in 1962, when he was 42 years old. In his final season, 1963, he hit a home run in his first at bat after becoming a grandfather. Musial was voted the Player of the Decade in 1956 for the period from 1946 to 1955, beating out stars such as Joe DiMaggio and Ted Williams. Inducted in 1969.

MAJOR LEAGUE TOTALS			
BA	H	HR	RBI
.331	3,630	475	1,951

(continued from page 67)

became a pitcher. Starting in center field for the 1946 Indians, his average lagged below .200 several weeks into the season. Player-manager Lou Boudreau moved him to the mound, inspiring a new career that resulted in seven 20-win seasons and a stellar .618 career winning percentage.

He cracked the starting rotation in mid-1947, and won 10 consecutive games. The following year, Lemon won 20 games and topped the American League with 293⅔ innings, 20 complete games, and 10 shutouts. In addition, he completed a no-hitter against the Tigers. Cleveland won the 1948 AL flag, and Lemon won both his World Series starts. He led the league in wins three times and complete games five times. Inducted in 1976.

MAJOR LEAGUE TOTALS			
W	L	ERA	K
207	128	3.23	1,277

JOCKO CONLAN

John Bertrand "Jocko" Conlan was the first umpire from the modern era selected to the Hall of Fame. Known for his trademark polka-dot bow tie, he had a quick wit and a sharp tongue and was one of the most respected umpires of all time. In his first big-league umpiring season, he ejected 26 men. He officiated for 27 seasons, working six All-Star Games, six World Series, and four playoffs. Inducted in 1974.

GEORGE KELL

An outstanding gloveman, George Clyde Kell also blazed the way for a new breed of third sackers who could also hit. In 1946, he began a string of eight straight .300 seasons. Kell won a batting title in 1949, edging Ted Williams by two-tenths of a point. Renowned for his glove, Kell retired with a .969 fielding average—a record that stood for 20 years. Inducted in 1983.

MAJOR LEAGUE TOTALS			
BA	H	HR	RBI
.306	2,054	78	870

WARREN SPAHN

Warren Edward Spahn won more than 20 games in 13 of the 17 years in which he had at least 30 starts, on his way to winning more games than any lefty in history. He was the best, and often the only good,

pitcher on two decades of Braves teams, from Boston to Milwaukee, as he led the league in wins a record eight times and complete games a record nine times.

After earning a Bronze Star and Purple Heart in World War II, Spahn established himself as a big-league star in 1947, winning 21 and leading the NL with a 2.33 ERA. In 1948, he teamed with Johnny Sain in the famous "Spahn and Sain and pray for rain" rotation. Sain won 24 games, Spahn 15, and the Braves won the pennant.

In 1949, Spahn led the National League in wins, complete games, innings, and strikeouts. He led again in wins and Ks the next year. Spahn won 22 games in 1951, a league-leading 23 in 1953, 21 in 1954, and 20 in 1956. When he began to lose some velocity on his fastball, Spahn compensated by developing new pitches and researching the league's batters.

Spahn's only two World Series appearances were splits with the Yankees in 1957 and 1958. He went on to win more than 20 games again in 1959, 1960, 1961, and 1963. Inducted in 1973.

MAJOR LEAGUE TOTALS			
W	L	ERA	K
363	245	3.09	2,583

JACKIE ROBINSON

During the first half of this century, a color line in America excluded African Americans from nearly every significant field of endeavor. The first high-profile integration came on a baseball diamond, and the first black man to cross the white lines was Jackie Robinson.

An outstanding athlete, Jack Roosevelt Robinson starred in four sports at UCLA. After his discharge from World War II, Robinson joined the Kansas City Monarchs of the Negro League. When approached by the Dodgers, Jackie was initially disbelieving and disin-terested—until he had a heart-to-heart talk with Dodgers owner Branch Rickey. Rickey chose Robinson as the first African American to join the major leagues for many reasons but most particularly for his strength of character. Jackie had to face the hatred and not fight back.

With the Dodgers in 1947, Robinson was Rookie of the Year. Jackie kept his cool despite overt racism early on. Eventually, he won over everybody.

Jackie won a batting title in 1949 with a .342 average and was named the league's MVP. Though he played just 10 seasons, he helped the Dodgers to six World Series. Robinson was the most devastating baserunner of his day and a fine basestealer. He had dangerous home run power and was exceptionally difficult to strike out. Inducted in 1962.

MAJOR LEAGUE TOTALS			
BA	H	HR	RBI
.311	1,518	137	734

BRANCH RICKEY

The rules of baseball have remained relatively stable through-out this century. Off the field, how-ever, revolutionary changes have taken place, and no man had a greater impact on what happened to baseball outside the diamond than Wesley Branch Rickey.

Not a great baseball player but well educated, Rickey moved into

management, first as field manager then as GM of the St. Louis Cardinals in 1917. It was as a club operator that Rickey was peerless. He had a keen eye for talent.

With the Cardinals in the 1920s, Rickey began to acquire minor-league clubs. With his own source of players, he could both stock the Cards and provide trade bait. By the time the Cards won their first pennant in 1926, they owned many clubs and kept acquiring more. Under Rickey, the Cardinals won six pennants.

Moving to Brooklyn in 1942, Rickey broke the color line by bringing Jackie Robinson to the Dodgers. Rickey also signed Roy Campanella and Don Newcombe out of the Negro Leagues, providing the Dodgers with three awesome talents that helped them dominate the NL in the 1950s.

Rickey's last venture in baseball was an attempt to launch a third major league in 1960, spurring the major-league expansion in the early 1960s. Inducted in 1967.

RED SCHOENDIENST

One of the best second basemen of the 1950s, Albert Fred Schoendienst teamed with shortstop Marty Marion to form one of baseball's best-ever double-play combinations.

Schoendienst hit better than .300 in six seasons. In 1957, he led the league in hits, becoming only the second man to do so after being traded midseason. Red's top batting average was .342 in 1953. He had good speed and was a fine doubles hitter. Inducted in 1989.

MAJOR LEAGUE TOTALS			
BA	H	HR	RBI
.289	2,449	84	773

RALPH KINER

Ralph McPherran Kiner won a National League-record seven straight home run titles. Only Babe Ruth has a career home run ratio better than Kiner's.

In 1946, Kiner became the Pirates left fielder, and his 23 home

runs led the league. In 1947, when the Pirates moved the left-field fence in 30 feet, Kiner took advantage by hitting 51 homers in 1947, 40 in 1948, and 54 in 1949. He walked 100 times or more in five straight seasons to post an excellent lifetime on-base average of .398, which in turn helped him to six seasons of at least 100 runs scored. The Pirates were usually in the cellar during Kiner's tenure, but he was recognized as one of the game's greatest stars. Inducted in 1975.

MAJOR LEAGUE TOTALS			
BA	H	HR	RBI
.279	1,451	369	1,015

HAPPY CHANDLER

Albert B. "Happy" Chandler's tenure as commissioner of baseball, from 1945 to 1951, was marked by wide extremes of strong action, inaction, and questionable action, all of which helped lead to his ouster at the end of his single term.

At the head of Happy's list of accomplishments stands the integration of baseball. Without Chandler's approval, Branch Rickey might not have been able to proceed with his plan to open the doors to black players. Inducted in 1982.

RICHIE ASHBURN

Richard Ashburn played in the same era as Willie, Mickey, and the

Duke, but he was in Philadelphia, while the other three enjoyed the spotlights of New York. While Ashburn's style involved hitting singles and getting on base, his northern colleagues swatted long home runs. Ashburn played in one World Series to Mays's four, Snider's six, and Mantle's dozen. No wonder Richie tended to be overlooked.

A classic leadoff hitter, Ashburn averaged 172 hits, 80 walks, and 88 runs over a 15-year career. He hit over .300 nine times, winning a pair of batting titles. Furthermore, he was a brilliant center fielder who recorded more than 6,000 putouts, with four seasons of 500 or more and another pair above 490. Though not blessed with a strong arm, he played shallow and used it wisely—his peg to home to nail Cal Abrams on the last day of 1950 won the Phils the pennant. Inducted in 1995.

MAJOR LEAGUE TOTALS			
BA	H	HR	RBI
.308	2,574	29	586

MICKEY MANTLE

T he most feared hitter on the most successful team in history, Mickey Charles Mantle overcame great pain in his quest to satisfy his fans, his father, and himself.

Mickey was the son of Mutt Mantle, a lead miner who dreamed of a good life for his son. A standout schoolboy player, Mickey was hampered by a serious football injury that caused osteomyelitis and nearly cost him his left leg—and his life.

Mickey opened the 1951 season as the Yanks' right fielder, but he was sent to the American Association in midseason. Discouraged, he wanted to quit baseball, but Mutt goaded him back on the path to stardom.

Mantle had enormous forearms and blazing speed, and he became a superb center fielder, taking over for Joe DiMaggio in 1952. Mantle

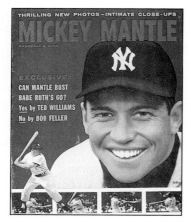

Mantle's popularity was so great, he was able to inspire special-issue magazines all by himself.

was possibly the fastest man in the game during his early years. In his best seasons, and there were many good ones, Mantle was simply a devastating player. He could run like the wind and hit tape-measure homers such as his famous 565-footer in Washington in 1953. He led the Yanks to 12 fall classics in 14 years, and seven world championships. He still holds the records for most homers, RBI, runs, walks, and strikeouts in World Series play. Mantle led the AL with 129 runs in 1954 and got his first home run title in 1955 with 37. He was a free

swinger who struck out often but could also take a walk, 10 times drawing at least 100.

In 1956, Mantle enjoyed one of the greatest seasons ever at the plate. He hit 52 homers with 130 RBI and a .353 average to win the Triple Crown. He also led the league with 132 runs and a .705 slugging percentage. He had 112 walks and won the first of three Most Valuable Player Awards. Mantle won MVP honors in 1957, hitting .365 with 34 homers, 94 RBI, 121 runs scored, and 146 bases on balls.

Mantle notched homer crowns in 1958 and 1960, then got into a duel with Roger Maris in 1961 to break Babe Ruth's single-season home run mark. While Maris's 61 was the winner, Mick led the league with a .687 slugging percentage, 132 runs scored, and 126 bases on balls. Mantle won an MVP Award in 1962 with a .321 average, 30 homers, and 89 RBI.

Mantle went public with his alcoholism late in his life and earned high marks for heroism as he nobly battled the cancer that would eventually take his life. Inducted in 1974.

MAJOR LEAGUE TOTALS			
BA	H	HR	RBI
.298	2,415	536	1,509

Yogi Berra

Lawrence Peter "Yogi" Berra was a mainstay of the most dominating baseball team in history, the New York Yankees of the late 1940s through early '60s. Although he never led the league in a single major offensive category, he won three Most Valuable Player Awards (just the third player to do so), and he played in 14 World Series.

Berra's malaprops and homespun wisdom captured the affections of baseball fans. Stocky and short, with a well-publicized penchant for comic books, Berra was also one of the most dangerous hitters in the American League.

Yogi didn't become the Bombers' No. 1 catcher until 1949. In 1950, he batted .322 with 28 homers and 124 RBI. Although his 1951 season wasn't as impressive (a .294 batting average, 27 home runs, and 88 RBI), he won his first MVP Award due to his great leadership behind the plate; then won consecutive MVP trophies in 1954 and 1955.

Berra worked to become a fine defensive catcher. He was a superb handler of pitchers and a wizard, for a catcher, at the double play. Berra owns a host of World Series records. He also managed the Yankees and the Mets to pennants. Inducted in 1972.

MAJOR LEAGUE TOTALS			
BA	H	HR	RBI
.285	2,150	358	1,430

Roy Campanella

Roy Campanella, along with Jackie Robinson and Don Newcombe, was a pioneering black ballplayer who bolstered a Dodger organization that, to this day, is acknowledged as one of the top teams in baseball history.

A Negro League star for nine years, Campanella was convinced to sign with the Dodger organization in 1946 and won MVP Awards in both of his minor-league seasons. Campy was a success from the day he arrived in Brooklyn in mid-1948. The stocky catcher had a rocket for an arm and a powerful bat and handled a legendary pitching staff to five pennants in 10 years. Campanella was a prime reason the 1950s Dodgers were the exceptional team in the NL. In 1951, Campanella won the first of three Most Valuable Player Awards, a feat accomplished by only a small group of stars. His next MVP season (1953) was among the best ever recorded by a catcher, as he led the

league with 142 RBI, clubbed 41 homers, scored 103 runs, and batted .312.

After a hand injury shortened his 1954 season, he rebounded in 1955 to win his third MVP Award. But nerve damage caused by the injury hampered his play in 1957. A return to form never happened. During the winter between the 1957 and 1958 seasons, Campanella was paralyzed in a car crash and never played again. Inducted in 1969.

MAJOR LEAGUE TOTALS			
BA	H	HR	RBI
.276	1,161	242	856

Duke Snider

In the 1950s, the Yankees had Mickey Mantle, the Giants had Willie Mays, and in Brooklyn, Duke Snider was king. In the four years the three shared New York headlines, Edwin Donald Snider had the

(continued on page 75)

WILLIE MAYS

Few players have combined grace, popularity, and accomplishment like Willie Howard Mays. He was a beautiful fielder, a tremendous power hitter, an outstanding outfield thrower, a canny baserunner, a huge drawing card, and a durable champion.

In 1951, Mays was batting .477 at Minneapolis of the American Association when Leo Durocher demanded that he be promoted to help the floundering Giants, who were 6-20. The New York front office published an apology in the Minneapolis paper, understanding the impression Willie had made on Millers fans.

Although Willie started out his major-league career 0-for-22, he had a galvanizing effect on the Giants. They came from 13½ games back to force a playoff with the front-running Dodgers, beating them on Bobby Thomson's home run. Mays hit 20 homers, perfected center field play, and won the Rookie of the Year Award. He also won the hearts of teammates and fans alike for his enthusiasm and good humor.

Mays served in the Army for most of 1952 and all of 1953. Had he played those years, Willie would have almost certainly broken Babe Ruth's lifetime home run record. In 1954, Willie returned to win the MVP Award, lead the league with a .345 average and a .667 slugging percentage, and hit 41 homers. His catch of a Vic Wertz drive in the Giants' World Series victory has become one of baseball's most treasured moments.

Willie led the NL in homers with 51 in 1955. He hit more than 35 homers 10 times and more than 40 homers six times, twice topping 50, and won five slugging crowns. To his power, average, arm, and defense, add speed: He won four stolen base crowns and three triples titles. In 1965, he won his second MVP Award by batting .317 with 52 homers and 112 RBI. Mays finished

Willie Mays made the cover of **Sport Parade** *magazine in 1964.*

among the top six in MVP voting an amazing 12 times.

Mays won a dozen Gold Gloves in a row for his outfield play. He retired with records for games, putouts, and chances for center fielders.

Willie showed true greatness in his longevity. At age 40, he led the league in walks, hit 18 homers, and was 23-for-26 as a basestealer. As a testimony to his batting skill, although he hit as high as .290 only once in his final eight seasons, his lifetime average remained above .300. He spent his final two seasons as a Met, back with the New Yorkers who missed him, and appeared in one final World Series. Inducted in 1979.

MAJOR LEAGUE TOTALS			
BA	H	HR	RBI
.302	3,283	660	1,903

(continued from page 73)
most homers and RBI of the three men, and he totaled more home runs and more RBI than any player in the 1950s.

The Duke played his first game for the Dodgers in the same week in 1947 that Jackie Robinson did. But Duke was sent back to the minors shortly thereafter. When he mastered the strike zone, Snider provided the left-handed power for the Boys of Summer. He hit .292 with 23 homers in 1949 and led the NL with 199 base hits while getting 31 homers in 1950. He led the league in runs scored in 1953, 1954, and 1955. He joined Babe Ruth and Ralph Kiner as the only men to ever hit at least 40 homers in five straight seasons (from 1953 to 1957). But the Dodgers' move to Los Angeles and the vast right field of the L.A. Coliseum ended Snider's streak in 1958.

The Duke was a regular on six Dodger pennant winners, turning in awesome World Series performances. He hit four homers twice in World Series competition. He was an outstanding center fielder with an amazingly powerful arm.

Snider ranks fourth on the all-time World Series home run list with 11. Inducted in 1980.

MAJOR LEAGUE TOTALS			
BA	H	HR	RBI
.295	2,116	407	1,333

ROBIN ROBERTS

Robin Evan Roberts won 20 or more games each season from 1950 to 1955. He pitched in the majors for 19 years, winning at least 10 games in all of the 14 seasons in which he had at least 30 starts.

In 1950, Roberts won 20 games, the first of six straight 20-win seasons. He was among league leaders in most categories that year. His 28-7 record in 1952 led the league by 10 wins and included the most NL wins in 50 years. From 1953 to '55, he led the NL with 23 wins a year; in games started from 1950 to '55; and in complete games from 1952 to '56. He also led the NL in Ks in 1953 and '54. Inducted in 1976.

MAJOR LEAGUE TOTALS			
W	L	ERA	K
286	245	3.41	2,357

WHITEY FORD

Edward Charles Ford was the ace for the 1950s Yanks. His .690 winning percentage is the best of any modern 200-game winner; his teams won 11 pennants and seven World

Series. Ford captured 15 Series records, including a streak of 33 scoreless innings.

After a 9-1 record in 1950, Ford spent two years in the military. When he returned, he sported a record of 18-6 to lead the Yankees to a fifth straight world championship.

During Ford's first 14 seasons, only twice did he post a record as low as three games over .500. He led the AL with 18 wins and 18 complete games in 1955. In 1956, he had the league's best ERA at 2.47. Manager Casey Stengel kept Ford under 250 innings a season, but when Ralph Houk took the reins in 1961, he unleashed Ford, who went an AL-top 25-4, winning the Cy Young.

Ford was a superb craftsman with excellent control. Although some of his pitches weren't legal, the threat of doctored balls was as good as throwing them. Inducted in 1974.

MAJOR LEAGUE TOTALS			
W	L	ERA	K
236	106	2.75	1,956

Chapter Six
MANIFEST DESTINY

Baseball's Changing Map

After years of status quo, baseball franchises began to shift in the 1950s. Air travel made cities across America accessible. With that in mind, in 1958 the Dodgers moved to Los Angeles and the Giants to San Francisco.

In an effort to thwart Branch Rickey's proposed upstart Continental League, the American League awarded a new franchise to Washington (after the original Senators moved to Minnesota) and placed another in Los Angeles for the 1961 season. The National League returned to New York with a 1962 expansion team and moved to Houston. Each new franchise cost its owners $2 million.

In the mid-1960s, the Houston Colt .45s changed their nickname to Astros after occupying the Astrodome, baseball's first domed ballpark, which featured artificial turf—and the Milwaukee Braves moved to Atlanta. In 1968, pitchers had become so dominating that batting averages fell, home run production was off, and there were sharp increases in the number of low-scoring games. Baseball executives, viewing those trends with alarm, decided to narrow the strike zone and lower the mound.

There was another round of expansion in 1969. Kansas City, which had lost the Athletics to Oakland in 1968, returned to the AL with the Royals while a new team was awarded to Seattle. The National League assigned a team to San Diego and went international by adding the Montreal Expos. Both leagues agreed to split into divisions, with divisional champions in a best-of-five playoff to determine World Series participants.

An advertising tab features right-hander Don Drysdale, one half of the lefty-righty duo that the Dodgers used to clobber the opposition with in the 1960s.

EDDIE MATHEWS

Edwin Lee Mathews is best remembered as teaming with Hank Aaron to form the Braves' one-two punch that dominated the National League in the 1950s and early 1960s. Mathews was the best-hit-ting third baseman in history before Mike Schmidt.

Mathews won his first home run title (with 47) his second year in the big leagues and his team's first in Milwaukee—1953. He provided power the next three seasons, ring-ing up 37 or more homers and 95 or more RBI from 1954 to 1956. In 1957, he batted .292 with 32 homers and 94 RBI as the Braves won the world championship. Two years later, in 1959, Mathews won the homer crown with 46 dingers.

Mathews hit at least 30 homers in 10 seasons, four times hitting more than 40. He led the league in walks four times, had 90 or more bases on balls nine times, and scored at least 95 runs in 10 straight seasons. Playing in the shadow of the great Hank Aaron may have obscured Mathews's performance, but together they hit 863 home runs, more than Babe Ruth and Lou Gehrig.

When Mathews first joined the Braves, he played the hot corner poorly, but he matured into a capable third baseman, leading the NL in putouts twice, assists three times, and fielding average once. He is eighth among third sackers in career double plays. Inducted in 1978.

MAJOR LEAGUE TOTALS			
BA	H	HR	RBI
.271	2,315	512	1,453

AL LOPEZ

Alfonso Raymond Lopez ranks fifth on the all-time list of most games as a catcher: 1,918. He applied the lessons he learned behind the plate to become one of the best managers in history.

Lopez finished first or second in each of his first nine seasons as a major-league skipper. In 1954, Lopez steered Cleveland to an AL-record 111 wins. His White Sox toppled the Yankees in 1959. Lopez retired from the helm with 1,410 victories and a .584 winning percentage in 17 seasons. Inducted in 1977.

MAJOR LEAGUE TOTALS		
W	L	PCT
1,410	1,004	.584

WARREN GILES

Warren Giles served as National League president from 1952 to 1969. He was intimately involved in the development of the farm system and, later, the scouting and signing of African-American and Latin-American players.

Giles oversaw the Boston Braves' move to Milwaukee in 1953. While that shift created some debate, it was nothing like the turmoil created in 1957 when the Dodgers and Giants headed for California. Inducted in 1979.

HOYT WILHELM

James Hoyt Wilhelm blazed the way for the modern relief specialist and was the first career reliever to enter the Hall of Fame. He pitched in more games than anyone else in history and retired with more relief wins than any other major-leaguer.

At age 16, Wilhelm studied a newspaper article describing the mechanics of throwing the knuckleball, and he eventually became a master. He was successful in his first pro season in 1942, but World War II intervened.

Hoyt didn't make the majors until 1952, with the Giants as a reliever. He burst out of nowhere to lead the National League with 71 games pitched, 15 relief wins, a 2.43 ERA, and an .833 winning percentage. In his first career at bat, he smashed a home run. In his second at bat, he smacked a triple. When Wilhelm retired 21 seasons later, he had totaled one career home run and one career triple. He led the league in appearances in 1953, and he notched 15 saves. In 1954, he had a 2.10 ERA and a league-best 12 relief wins. The Giants went on to win the World Series that year; Wilhelm recorded a save in his only postseason appearance.

(continued on page 79)

HANK AARON

O n April 23, 1954, Hank Aaron hit the first of his 755 major-league home runs—the most of any player in history. Henry Louis Aaron grew up one of eight children in Mobile, Alabama, and learned the art of baseball by hitting bottle caps with a broomstick. When he was only 17, he was playing for the Negro League Indianapolis Clowns. The Braves signed Aaron in 1952, and he batted .336 in the Northwest League. In 1953, he was one of three players to integrate the South Atlantic League, which he led with

a .362 average, 125 RBI, and 115 runs scored. Hank inherited the left-field job in Milwaukee in 1954 when Bobby Thomson broke his ankle.

Aaron had an all-around game that was second to none. He became one of the top outfielders in the game. He was consistent and careful and deadly. His quick wrists were the stuff of legend. In 1956, he led the National League with a .328 batting average. In 1957, he won the National League MVP Award with a .322 batting average, 44 home runs, and 132 RBI. The Braves won the pennant that year, and then went on to defeat a powerful Yankees team in the World Series. Hank hit .393 with three home runs in the seven games. Although the Braves remained a strong team for many years, the 1957 championship was Aaron's only world title.

On April 8, 1974, Aaron broke Babe Ruth's lifetime home run record. Racism, combined with fans' reverence for the Babe, added to the difficulty of that monumental task. Always a quiet, serious professional, Henry withstood the burden and scrutiny of an all-out media assault with calm and restraint. "Thank God it's over," he said after the record-breaking game.

Aaron won a record eight total-bases titles, en route to the all-time record of 6,856 total bases. He slugged over .500 18 times and bat-

The trophy Hank received for breaking Babe Ruth's career home run mark.

ted .300 14 times. He drove in 89 or more runs in 13 consecutive seasons and 17 times in all, finishing his career with an all-time-best 2,297 runs batted in. He hit 30 or more homers in 15 seasons. Aaron ranks third in games played and had the second-most at bats of any player in history, and he had taken all those swings as perhaps the greatest right-handed hitter in history. Pitcher Curt Simmons said, "Throwing a fastball by Henry Aaron is like trying to sneak sunrise past a rooster." Inducted in 1982.

MAJOR LEAGUE TOTALS			
BA	H	HR	RBI
.305	3,771	755	2,297

(continued from page 77)

Wilhelm stayed in the game until he was 49 years old. From 1962 to 1968, he posted ERAs below 2.00 in six of the seven years. Inducted in 1985.

MAJOR LEAGUE TOTALS			
W	L	SV	ERA
143	122	227	2.52

ERNIE BANKS

Ernest Banks's reputation as a goodwill ambassador should not obscure his great playing ability. He was a fine fielding shortstop and a power hitter who had an unbridled enthusiasm for the game.

After two seasons as a Negro Leaguer, Banks became the Cubs' everyday shortstop in 1954, hitting .275 with 19 home runs and 79 RBI. In 1955, he batted .295 and clubbed 44 home runs with five grand slams, a single-season record he shares with Jim Gentile. He was the first player from a sub-.500

team to be voted Most Valuable Player when he led the league with 47 home runs (the most ever by a shortstop) and 129 RBI in 1958. The following year, Banks became the first NL player to win back-to-back MVP Awards.

A fine shortstop for nine seasons, Banks won a Gold Glove in 1960. His 105 double plays in 1954 is still a rookie record. He was an 11-time All-Star.

Banks hit more than 40 homers five times and had more than 100 RBI in eight seasons. Although the Cubs failed to win a pennant during Ernie's 19-year career, he earned the title "Mr. Cub." He was well known for his love of the game and his credo, "Let's play two." Inducted in 1977.

MAJOR LEAGUE TOTALS			
BA	H	HR	RBI
.274	2,583	512	1,636

AL KALINE

The career of Albert William Kaline, who joined the Detroit Tigers as an 18-year-old boy and retired a 40-year-old legend, has a storybook quality. He hit for average, hit for power, and was a near-perfect defensive player with an arm like a rocket launcher. He is among the best loved of Detroit stars.

Because of the bonus rule, Kaline never played an inning of minor-league ball. He pinch-hit the day he signed, right out of high

school. In his second full season, 1955, Kaline proved he was a major-league hitter. He won the batting title that season, hitting .340 with a league-high 200 hits and 27 home runs. He finished a close second in the MVP vote. Al batted .314 in 1956, with 194 base hits, 27 homers, and a career-high 128 RBI.

From 1957 to 1967, Kaline batted from .278 to .327, with 18 to 25 homers and 70 to 100 RBI. The Tigers jelled in 1968, winning the pennant, but a broken leg held Kaline to 102 games. In the World Series, Tigers manager Mayo Smith gambled that outfielder Mickey Stanley could handle shortstop so Al could play right field. The gamble paid off when Kaline batted .379, slugged .655, and drove in eight runs as the Tigers won their first world championship since 1945. Inducted in 1980.

MAJOR LEAGUE TOTALS			
BA	H	HR	RBI
.297	3,007	399	1,583

HARMON KILLEBREW

The top right-handed home run hitter in AL history, Harmon Killebrew had more than 40 home runs in eight seasons and more than 100 RBI in nine seasons.

Killebrew was a bonus baby, so he didn't get a chance to play full-time for the Senators until 1959. But "Killer" was ready when he played as a regular in 1959, leading the league with 42 home runs during his first full season. He hit 31 the next year. In 1961, when the Senators became the Minnesota Twins, this dead pull hitter hit 46 home runs for his new fans, but that was the year Roger Maris went on his spree. Killebrew led the league in 1962, 1963, and 1964, hitting 142 home runs in the three seasons and driving in 333 runs. The Twins rocketed to first place in 1965 with 102 wins, though Killer had one of his poorest years due to an injury, and the Twins lost the World Series.

Killebrew had established himself as a major star with his consistent slugging. He won the AL MVP Award in 1969 when he hit 49 homers and drove in 140 runs and drew 145 walks, leading the league with a .430 on-base average. His walk totals were impressive and, though Killebrew drew criticism for his less-than-impressive batting averages, his on-base averages were usually among the best in the league. Inducted in 1984.

MAJOR LEAGUE TOTALS			
BA	H	HR	RBI
.256	2,086	573	1,584

WALTER ALSTON

Walter Emmons Alston was at the helm of the Dodgers for 23 years—from the team's mid-1950s battles with the Yankees to its mid-1970s races with the Big Red Machine. Alston led the Dodgers to seven pennants and four World Series victories.

After winning pennants in 1952 and 1953, Brooklyn manager Chuck

Dressen was fired when he demanded a multiyear contract. Alston was the surprise choice as Dressen's replacement, and Walt accepted one-year contracts for the next 23 years. In contrast to the other New York managers of the 1950s, Alston was a quiet, businesslike man. As a field general, he was in control. He was a devotee of bunts, the hit-and-run, intentional passes, stolen bases, platooning, pinch hitters, and using his entire roster. He also won two pennants in Brooklyn, and when the team went to Los Angeles he rebuilt the Dodgers around pitching and defense. He won five more flags in L.A. Inducted in 1983.

MAJOR LEAGUE TOTALS		
W	L	PCT
2,040	1,613	.558

SANDY KOUFAX

Sanford Koufax put together one of the most dominating stretches of pitching in baseball history. Over a five-year span, he led the NL in ERA five times and compiled a 111-34 record before arthritis forced him to retire at age 30.

In his early seasons, his bursts of brilliance were surrounded by intervals of wildness. It wasn't until 1961 spring training, when catcher Norm Sherry advised his pitcher to slow his delivery, throw off-speed, and relax, that Koufax came into his own. Sandy recorded his first plus-.500 record and led the league in

Ks with the eye-popping total of 269. In 1962, despite a circulatory ailment, he was 14-7 with a league-leading 2.54 ERA, and he pitched a no-hitter.

The 1963 season was his triumph. Koufax went 25-5, topping the NL with 25 wins, a 1.88 ERA, 11 shutouts, and 306 strikeouts. He won both the MVP and Cy Young Awards and tossed his second no-hitter. In 1964, he was 19-5 with a league-best 1.74 ERA. That year, a deteriorating arthritic condition in his left arm first became conspicuous. With the help of cortisone shots and ice for two more seasons, Koufax won Cy Young Awards in 1965 and 1966. He had league-best ERAs of 2.04 and 1.73, and he won 26 and 27 games, respectively. Koufax also tossed two more no-hitters, including a perfect game. Inducted in 1972.

MAJOR LEAGUE TOTALS			
W	L	ERA	K
165	87	2.76	2,396

DON DRYSDALE

Donald Scott Drysdale combined a wicked fastball with a fierce demeanor to be one of the most intimidating hurlers of the period. He teamed with Sandy Koufax to form one of the top lefty-righty duos of all time.

Drysdale joined the Dodgers in 1956, where he was tutored in the fine art of pitching inside by Sal "The Barber" Maglie. In 1957, he was 17-9 with a 2.69 ERA. Don slumped in the team's first season in Los Angeles, but the next two seasons he led the NL in strikeouts.

In 1962, he went 25-9, leading the league in wins and strikeouts and earning the Cy Young Award. From 1962 to 1965, he averaged more than 21 wins per year as the Dodgers won two world championships. In 1965, Drysdale not only went 23-12, but he hit .300 with

seven home runs, tying the record for pitchers. Inducted in 1984.

MAJOR LEAGUE TOTALS			
W	L	ERA	K
209	166	2.95	2,486

JIM BUNNING

James Paul Bunning was the model of professional consistency. He never appeared in a postseason game, but he won 20 games once and 19 and 17 games three times each.

After two part-time and unspectacular seasons with Detroit, Bunning went to winter ball and learned a slider. His slider became one of the toughest ever: His first full season he used it to win 20 games, leading the AL in wins. He also notched his first no-hitter that year.

In 1964, when the Giants and Bunning's Phillies were locked in a

tight race for first place, Bunning threw a perfect game against the Mets. It took him just 90 pitches to shut the Mets down without a baserunner. His perfecto was the first regular-season major-league perfect game since 1922 and the first ever in the National League.

Bunning retired as the first modern era pitcher to win 100 games and fan 1,000 men in both leagues. Inducted in 1996.

MAJOR LEAGUE TOTALS			
W	L	ERA	K
224	184	3.27	2,855

ROBERTO CLEMENTE

Roberto Clemente y Walker had one of the strongest outfield arms in history, won four batting titles, and notched 3,000 career hits.

In 1955, the Pirates drafted Clemente away from the Dodgers.

Clemente joined the Pirates that year, and by 1960, he was a star, hitting .314 for the champion Bucs. He raised his game another notch in 1961, hitting .351, the first of five times he hit above .340. He won National League MVP honors in 1966.

No one who saw Clemente throw the ball could forget the power and accuracy of those throws. His arm was a deadly weapon, and he could unleash the ball from impossible angles and distances. He won Gold Gloves every year from 1961 through 1972. He has perhaps the greatest defensive reputation of any right fielder in history.

Although Clemente was troubled by a bad back, bone chips, and shoulder troubles throughout his career, he posted the highest batting average for the decade of the 1960s with a .328 mark. Clemente felt a duty to his fans, particularly his countrymen. He once said, "A country without idols is nothing." Clemente was an idol for many people in many countries.

On December 31, 1972, he was on a cargo plane from Puerto Rico airlifting emergency relief supplies for earthquake-torn Nicaragua. The plane crashed off the coast of Puerto Rico—there were no survivors. Inducted in 1973.

MAJOR LEAGUE TOTALS			
BA	H	HR	RBI
.317	3,000	240	1,305

BROOKS ROBINSON

Brooks Calbert Robinson revolutionized the third base position. He was a soft-handed, accurate-armed man who did with reflexes and intelligence what quickness and a strong arm couldn't accomplish alone. He won the Gold Glove 16 times and earned 15 straight All-Star Game starting assignments. Upon his retirement, Robinson held almost every major fielding record for third basemen, including most games (2,870), highest fielding average (.971), most putouts (2,697), most assists (6,205), and most double plays (618).

By 1960, Robinson was the regular Oriole third baseman, and he remained there 18 years. Just a respectable offensive performer during the next four years, in 1964, Robinson batted .317 with 28 homers and a league-leading 118 RBI. His offense and defense earned him AL MVP honors.

Robinson's work in the 1970 World Series earned him Series MVP honors; he hit .429 with two homers and a highlight reel full of defensive gems. In 23 big-league seasons, he had more than 20 homers six times and more than 80 RBI eight times. Robinson led American League third basemen in fielding average in 11 seasons, including five years and then four years consecutively. He also led circuit hot corner men in assists eight times, putouts and double plays three times, and total chances per game twice. Inducted in 1983.

MAJOR LEAGUE TOTALS			
BA	H	HR	RBI
.276	2,848	268	1,357

LUIS APARICIO

While shortstop Luis Ernesto Aparicio y Montiel patrolled American League infields from the mid-1950s to the 1970s, he was widely regarded as one of the best fielders at that position the game had ever seen. With Nellie Fox, he gave the White Sox one of the best keystone combinations ever.

Aparicio was the catalyst of a "Go-Go Sox" team that challenged the Yankees for dominance in the 1950s. In 1959, the Sox finally won the flag. All-Star Aparicio and keystone partner Fox each led the league at their positions in putouts, assists, and fielding percentage. Fox won the Most Valuable Player Award, and Luis was second.

Aparicio's 56 steals in 1959 not only led the league but represented a new level of performance that left the rest of the league in the dust. He posted stolen base totals of 51, 53, 31, 40, and 57, respectively, over the next five seasons; only one rival swiped more than 30 during that time. He won nine consecutive stolen base titles, a record that has never been broken.

Aparicio was unparalleled as a defensive player. He played more games at shortstop (2,581), was involved in more double plays (1,553), and threw out more men than any shortstop in history. He won nine Gold Gloves in three decades. Inducted in 1984.

MAJOR LEAGUE TOTALS			
BA	H	HR	RBI
.262	2,677	83	791

FRANK ROBINSON

Frank Robinson was the first player to win Most Valuable Player Awards in both leagues and was the first African American to gain a managerial berth in major-league baseball.

Robinson earned Rookie of the Year honors with Cincinnati in 1956, leading the league with 122 runs and hitting .290 with 38 homers, the home run total tying a National League rookie record. He was a fine defensive outfielder, winning a Gold Glove in 1958, and very quick on the bases. Robinson led the Reds to a pennant in 1961, leading the league with a .611 slugging percentage. He also batted .323 with 37 homers, 117 runs scored, 124 RBI, and 22 stolen bases. He was named National League Most Valuable Player. In 1962, he led the NL in slugging percentage for the third consecutive year.

In 1966, when Robinson was 30 years old, the Reds traded him to the Baltimore Orioles. There, he won the Triple Crown, became the only baseball player ever to win Most Valuable Player Awards in both leagues, and helped the Orioles beat the Dodgers in the World Series. His team won three straight pennants from 1968 to '70 and took home another championship in 1970.

In 1975, Robinson became the first African-American manager in baseball when he was named player-manager of the Indians. He batted over .300 nine times, swatted more than 30 homers 11 different times, and had more than 100 RBI in six seasons. Inducted in 1982.

MAJOR LEAGUE TOTALS			
BA	H	HR	RBI
.294	2,943	586	1,812

WILLIE McCOVEY

The "other" Willie on the 1960s San Francisco Giants, Willie Lee McCovey was one of the great sluggers of the decade, averaging 30 homers each year and leading the league in round-trippers three times and homer percentage four times.

After being called up to the Giants for the last 52 games of the 1959 season, "Stretch" belted 13 homers with a .354 average and was named National League Rookie of the Year. For the next five years he was forced to share playing time with Orlando Cepeda.

The Giants won the pennant in 1962. In the final inning of the World Series, McCovey hit a line drive—"the hardest ball I ever hit," he said—directly at Yankees second baseman Bobby Richardson. A hit to either side would have given the Giants the championship, and McCovey would have been hailed as the hero.

McCovey won the National League MVP Award in 1969, the middle year in a three-year span of outstanding production. Inducted in 1986.

MAJOR LEAGUE TOTALS			
BA	H	HR	RBI
.270	2,211	521	1,555

JUAN MARICHAL

Juan Antonio Marichal y Sanchez won more games than any other

pitcher during the 1960s, with 191 victories notched. In addition, he was the greatest control pitcher of his time—he walked just 709 men in more than 3,500 innings—with a delivery that defied logic. The timing oddities and whirl of motion that resulted from his high-kick windup baffled major-league hitters for 16 seasons.

Called up to San Francisco in 1960, Marichal was immediately effective: He notched a 6-2 record with a 2.66 ERA. In 1963, Marichal led the National League in wins, going 25-8. When he lost a game that year to Sandy Koufax, Marichal countered by pitching a no-hitter against Houston in his next start. He also encountered Warren Spahn on the mound, each going all the way in a 16-inning Giants win.

The 1963 season was the first of six 20-win campaigns in seven years for "Manito," who posted ERAs under 3.00 in each season. He finished in the top three in wins five times in the 1960s and also finished in the top three in ERA three times. Inducted in 1983.

MAJOR LEAGUE TOTALS			
W	L	ERA	K
243	142	2.89	2,303

BOB GIBSON

In the 1960s, when power pitchers ruled the game, few were as dominant as Robert Gibson. He was an exciting and successful World Series performer as well.

In 1961, when new Cards manager Johnny Keane put Gibson in the starting rotation to stay, Bob led the league in walks but still won 13 games. The following season, he struck out 208 hitters in the first of nine 200-K seasons. No pitcher posted more strikeouts that decade. In 1964, he was 19-12 and led the Cardinals to a World Series title.

A star in the World Series, Gibson won a National League-record seven games, losing only two as the Cards won world championships in 1964 and 1967 and lost in 1968: In the 1964 fall classic, he won two games and notched an ERA of 3.00; in 1967, he won three championship games.

In 1968, Gibson won both the MVP and Cy Young Awards. His record was 22-9, with an NL-record 1.12 ERA and a league-best 268 strikeouts. He pitched 13 shutouts, and one-fifth of all his decisions were shutouts. In the World Series that year, Gibson had a single-game-record 17 strikeouts.

Gibson won another Cy Young Award in 1970. A tremendous athlete, he also had 24 lifetime home runs and nine consecutive Gold Gloves. Inducted in 1981.

MAJOR LEAGUE TOTALS			
W	L	ERA	K
251	174	2.91	3,117

CARL YASTRZEMSKI

A great hitter for several seasons and a very good hitter for many years, Carl Michael Yastrzemski performed the impossible: replacing Ted Williams.

Yaz was moved into Williams's left-field spot in 1961. In his third season, he won his first batting title with a .321 average, demonstrating good power and a good eye. In 1965, he led the AL with a .536 slugging percentage and 45 doubles and in 1966 led the circuit with 39 doubles.

The Red Sox, a ninth-place team in 1966, won the pennant on the last day of the 1967 season in the tightest race in American League history. Yaz won the Triple Crown that year, hitting .326 with a career-best 44 homers and 121 RBI, the last man to win a Triple Crown. In the final two weeks of the season, he hit .522 with five home runs. Yaz was devastating in the final series against the Twins, going 7-for-8 and playing stellar defense. Deservedly, he was named the AL MVP.

In 1968, Yastrzemski won the batting title with the lowest average ever, .301. In 1969 and 1970 he hit 40 homers. He had an upright, distinctive stance, his bat almost straight up-and-down. Of his successor, Ted Williams said Yaz "reminded me of myself at that age—I mean he positively quivered waiting for that next pitch." Inducted in 1989.

MAJOR LEAGUE TOTALS			
BA	H	HR	RBI
.285	3,419	452	1,844

Chapter Seven

NEW FRONTIER

Growth and Prosperity

I n the first year of divisional play, the 1969 "Miracle Mets" won the world championship seven years after having the worst record of any expansion club. The other three teams in the playoffs that year—Baltimore, Minnesota, and Atlanta—had shifted from their original locales.

The greatest shift in the way the game was played occurred in 1973, when the American League unilaterally adopted the designated hitter. That year, the composite league batting average rose 20 points, to .259. The following year, Hank Aaron became baseball's career home run king, Mike Marshall became the first relief pitcher to win the Cy Young Award, and Lou Brock broke Maury Wills's single-season stolen base record.

While records were falling on the field, players were reaping the benefits of a salary explosion fueled by arbitration and free agency. In 1976, an arbitrator's ruling regarding the option clause in the standard player's contract made free agency a reality. A new Basic Agreement between players and owners created a complex re-entry system granting free agency to veterans with more than six years of service. Bidding wars sparked by the advent of free agency sent baseball salaries on a steep upward spiral after 1976. The average major-league salary had jumped from $34,000 in 1971 to $185,000 in 1980 and $597,537 in 1990. Mike Schmidt peaked at a perfect time. In the 1980s alone, Schmidt earned $17,076,738—more than the combined incomes of the five U.S. presidents who held office during Mike's career.

Billy Williams's jersey as a member of the 1970s Oakland A's. He was the model of consistency. In his first 13 full seasons, he never collected fewer than 20 home runs or 84 RBI.

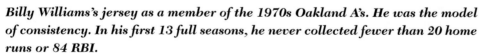

BILLY WILLIAMS

Billy Leo Williams, best remembered for his flawless swing, was a model of the quiet, consistent star. He established a National League record by playing in 1,117 consecutive games. He had more than 20 homers and more than 80 RBI in 13 consecutive seasons.

No less a baseball luminary than Rogers Hornsby loved Billy's swing and urged the Cubs to promote him to the bigs. In 1961, Williams's 25 homers and .278 average earned him NL Rookie of the Year honors.

He never fanned more than 84 times in a season, and he drove in or scored more than 100 runs eight times. From 1962 to 1969, his batting average hovered between .276 and .315, and he had 21 to 34 homers, 84 to 108 RBI, and 87 to 115 runs scored. Williams batted

over the .300 barrier five times and topped 200 hits in a season three times. Inducted in 1987.

MAJOR LEAGUE TOTALS			
BA	H	HR	RBI
.290	2,711	426	1,475

LOU BROCK

In 1964, the Chicago Cubs traded Louis Clark Brock to the Cards. Hitting .251 for the Cubs at the time, Brock went on to hit .348 the rest of the season as the Cardinals charged from behind to win the NL pennant. Brock ruled left field in St. Louis for 15 more seasons.

In 1965, Brock scored 107 runs and stole 63 bases, then swiped an NL-high 74 bases in 1966, getting his first stolen base crown. Lou led the Cards to two consecutive NL pennants in 1967 and 1968, topping the NL with 113 runs in 1967. In 1968, he led the circuit with 46

doubles and 14 triples. In each of those World Series, he hit over .400 and stole seven bases.

Brock led the NL in swipes from 1966 to 1969 and again from 1971 to 1974. In 1970 and 1971, he had more than 200 base hits and 100 runs scored each season, leading the NL with 126 runs in 1971. In 1974, a 35-year-old Brock stole 118 bases, breaking Maury Wills's 1962 single-season stolen base record of 104. Brock stole his 893rd base in 1977, breaking Ty Cobb's career record. In 1979, Brock's final season, he batted .304 at age 40 and garnered his 3,000th hit. Brock earned eight stolen base titles, scored more than 90 runs 10 times, batted .300 in eight seasons, and had more than 200 base hits four times. Inducted in 1985.

MAJOR LEAGUE TOTALS			
BA	H	HR	RBI
.293	3,023	149	900

TOM YAWKEY

In 1933, at age 30, Thomas Yawkey bought the Red Sox for $1.5 million and spared nothing in his attempt to bring a world championship to Boston. Although the Red Sox won pennants in 1946, 1967, and 1975, they lost each World Series in seven games.

Yawkey was very popular with his players. Joe Cronin said Yawkey "was not only the team owner, he was the team's No. 1 fan." Inducted in 1980.

WILLIE STARGELL

Wilver Dornel Stargell was one of the most potent power hitters of his time, a mainstay of the Pittsburgh Pirates for 21 years, and among the all-time leaders in home runs, slugging, and RBI.

Stargell took over left field for the Bucs in 1963. He started a string of 13 straight 20-homer seasons in 1964. It was after the Pirates moved to Three Rivers Stadium in 1970 that the country took notice of Willie. After a good season in 1970, Stargell exploded in 1971. The Pirates won the pennant again; Willie led the league with 48 homers and had 125 RBI. In 1973, Willie led the league with a .646 slugging percentage, 43 doubles, 44 homers, and 119 RBI. He is the only man to hit two balls out of Dodger Stadium, and his 296 homers were the most in the 1970s.

In 1979, Stargell led the Bucs to the world championship. Though

he played in just 126 games, he hit 32 homers and .281, and then hit over .400 with five homers in the playoffs and Series. He tied with St. Louis first baseman Keith Hernandez in the voting for the NL MVP Award and won both the NLCS and World Series MVPs. Stargell was the acknowledged leader of his team, noted for his character as well as his stats. Inducted in 1988.

MAJOR LEAGUE TOTALS			
BA	H	HR	RBI
.282	2,232	475	1,540

GAYLORD PERRY

Gaylord Jackson Perry—the only pitcher in history to win the Cy Young Award in both leagues—fooled hitters and umpires for 22 years, pitching for eight different teams. An admitted proponent of the spitball, he titled his autobiography *Me and the Spitter*. He contended that he rarely threw it,

maintaining that the belief that he might use a spitball was enough to put the hitter at a disadvantage. He heightened suspicion by his odd, herky-jerky delivery.

Perry won 314 games with a remarkable 3.11 ERA while playing on only one pennant-winning club. His brother Jim had 215 career wins, and the brothers' 529 total wins was the highest until the Niekro brothers surpassed them in 1987. Gaylord's 3,534 strikeouts rank him number six on the all-time list, and his 5,350⅓ innings pitched are in history's top ten. Inducted in 1991.

MAJOR LEAGUE TOTALS			
W	L	ERA	K
314	265	3.11	3,534

JOE MORGAN

Little Joe made the Big Red Machine go. Joe Leonard Morgan is best remembered as the catalyst

for the world champion Reds of 1975 and 1976. He played more games at second base than anyone but Eddie Collins.

In 1965, while with Houston, the 5'7" second baseman hit .271 with 14 home runs, 100 runs scored, and an NL-leading 97 walks, finishing second in the Rookie of the Year voting. He scored 94 runs in 1969, 102 in 1970, and 87 in 1971. Swapped to the Reds in a blockbuster deal, Morgan showed even more power. He hit 16 homers in 1972, 26 in 1973, and 22 in 1974. His walk totals those three years were 115, 111, and 120, respectively, and he scored 122, 116, and 107 runs.

Morgan was the only second sacker in baseball history to win back-to-back MVP Awards, in 1975 and 1976. In 1975, he batted .327 with 17 homers, 107 runs scored, 94 RBI, 67 stolen bases, and a league-best 132 bases on balls as the Reds won 108 games. Morgan

batted .320 with 27 homers, 113 runs scored, 111 RBI, 60 swipes, and 114 walks in 1976.

A steady fielder, Morgan won five straight Gold Gloves from 1973 to 1977. He led the NL in walks four times and runs once. Inducted in 1990.

MAJOR LEAGUE TOTALS			
BA	H	HR	RBI
.271	2,517	268	1,133

PHIL NIEKRO

Only the second knuckleballer to reach the Hall, Phil Niekro had a career that was notable more for longevity than for brilliance or dominance.

Although he started throwing the knuckler when he was 10 years old, it took seven minor-league seasons to perfect it. When he made the Braves in 1967, he led the NL in ERA, then began a streak in which he started at least 30 games 18 years straight (not including the 1981 strike year).

Niekro started more than 40 games each year from 1977 to '79 and led the NL in complete games with 20 or more each of those seasons. Plagued by a lack of support throughout his career, his 49 shutout losses are the third most in major-league history. When he won 21 games for the Braves in 1979, Niekro became just the second NL pitcher since 1901 to top 20 for a last-place team. But with 20 losses that year as well, he became the

first NL pitcher in 73 years to do a 20-20.

Released by the Braves at age 44, Niekro won 16 games in consecutive Yankee seasons. His 121 victories after turning 40 are the most in baseball history. With his brother Joe's 221 lifetime wins, the pair won more games than any other brothers in history. Inducted in 1997.

MAJOR LEAGUE TOTALS			
W	L	ERA	K
318	274	3.35	3,342

CATFISH HUNTER

James Augustus Hunter never pitched in the minors. He went from a simple 19-year-old in Kansas City to a Cy Young Award winner and the richest player in baseball.

Despite a perfect game in 1968, Hunter was just 30-36 lifetime when the team moved to Oakland. Catfish won 18 games in 1970 and then 21 in 1971, the first of five straight seasons in which he passed 20 wins. The A's became a power-house. Catfish's good fastball, guile, and pinpoint control won him 21, 21, and 25 games from 1972 to 1974; he lost a combined total of 24. He was 4-0 in those three World Series. His 1974 season earned him Cy Young honors as he posted a 25-12 record and a league-leading 2.49 ERA. When A's owner Charlie Finley failed to pay an insurance premium required in Hunter's contract, Catfish was

awarded free agency. All baseball was startled by the $3.75 million George Steinbrenner gave him for five years with the Yanks.

Catfish was 23-14 in his first year in pinstripes in 1975, and he led the league with 30 complete games and 328 innings. The Yankees won pennants in 1976, 1977, and 1978, but Hunter was just 38-30. With a lifetime record of 224-166 and a 3.26 ERA, Catfish fanned at least 100 batters in 11 consecutive seasons—finishing with 2,012 Ks—and never walked more than 85 in a season. Inducted in 1987.

MAJOR LEAGUE TOTALS			
W	L	ERA	K
224	166	3.26	2,012

JIM PALMER

The image of James Alvin Palmer as a pitchman for men's underwear tends to diminsh the record of the

Baltimore right-hander. Palmer won 20 games in eight seasons, won 15 games a dozen times, and allowed fewer than three earned runs a game 10 times.

Palmer gained his first bit of fame at age 20 by shutting out the Dodgers in Game 2 of the 1966 World Series. He missed most of the next two seasons with an arm injury, but came back after surgery in 1969 to win 16 games and lose only four, leading the AL with an .800 winning percentage. In 1970, he began a streak of four consecutive 20-win seasons. He led the league with a 2.40 ERA, going 22-9 for the 1973 Orioles to win his first Cy Young Award. In 1975, he led the AL with a 2.09 ERA and 23 victories to win his second Cy Young. He led the league in victories in 1976 (earning another Cy Young) and 1977, and he had 20 wins in 1978.

Jim subscribed to the theory that most batters couldn't handle his high, tight fastballs, and he was right. Despite various injuries, he

led the league in innings pitched four times. His Orioles won the AL East from 1969 to 1971 and in 1973, 1974, and 1979.

MAJOR LEAGUE TOTALS			
W	L	ERA	K
268	152	2.86	2,212

FERGUSON JENKINS

A master of control, Ferguson Arthur Jenkins never walked more than 83 hitters in a season. He is the only pitcher in baseball history to fan more than 3,000 batters while walking fewer than 1,000.

After two years in the Phils and Cubs bullpens, Ferguson was promoted to starter by Cub manager Leo Durocher at the end of the 1966 season, and he responded with two complete games. In 1967, he was 20-13 with a 2.80 ERA, the first of six consecutive 20-win seasons. He led the NL with 40 starts in 1968, going 20-15. He tied a major-league record by losing five decisions by the score of 1-0.

Jenkins's best season with the Cubs was 1971, when he led the league with 325 innings pitched and 24 wins and posted a 2.77 ERA to earn the Cy Young Award. He was 20-12 in 1972, but after slipping in 1973, he was sent to Texas.

Fergie had one more outstanding season. In 1974, he led the American League with a career-high 25 wins, lost 12, and fanned 225. Though he never won 20 games again, he continued to pitch

effectively. Jenkins led the league in strikeouts in 1969 and fanned more than 200 six times. Like other control pitchers, he gave up many homers; the 484 he allowed are the second most in history. Inducted in 1991.

MAJOR LEAGUE TOTALS			
W	L	ERA	K
284	226	3.34	3,192

TOM SEAVER

When George Thomas Seaver won 25 games to spirit the New York Mets to a stunning pennant in 1969, he earned the nickname "Tom Terrific." His 25 wins also set a Mets record that still stands.

Seaver was the Mets staff ace for 10 seasons. On three occasions (1969, 1973, and 1975) he won the Cy Young Award, and he twice hurled the Mets to a pennant. The team's second flag came in 1973 when Seaver earned his second Cy Young honor despite winning just

19 games. Seaver's stats that year were bolstered by both the NL ERA and strikeout crowns. In all, Seaver paced the senior circuit five times in whiffs. The last occasion, in 1976, marked the ninth consecutive season in which Seaver had fanned at least 200 hitters—a major-league record.

During the 1977 season, to the shock of Mets fans, Seaver was traded to Cincinnati. Although he twice led the NL in winning percentage, Seaver failed to bring the Reds a pennant. After six years in Cincinnati, he was reacquired by the Mets before the 1983 season but was drafted away by the White Sox. Seaver retired with a .603 career winning percentage, the highest of any 300-game winner in the past half-century. Inducted in 1992.

MAJOR LEAGUE TOTALS			
W	L	ERA	K
311	205	2.86	3,640

JOHNNY BENCH

Johnny Lee Bench was the best offensive and defensive catcher in baseball for a decade and a cornerstone of Cincinnati's Big Red Machine in the 1970s. In fact, Bench, the first player from the draft inducted into the Hall of Fame, ranks among the greatest catchers in baseball history.

He hit with enough power to lead the National League in homers twice and in RBI three times. Bench monopolized the Gold Glove Award from 1968 through 1977. His arm, which would have been an asset in any era, became even more important when artificial turf gave baserunners an extra step.

Bench's one-handed catching method gave him greater mobility and allowed him to use his throwing arm more effectively. National League Rookie of the Year in 1968, he won MVP Awards in 1970 and 1972. When in 1970, at age 22, he led the league with 45 homers and

148 RBI, Bench became the youngest man ever to win the MVP Award. His second MVP Award came for a season in which he hit .270 with 40 homers and 125 RBI.

Bench's 327 homers as a catcher constituted a record when he retired after the 1983 season, and he rates near the top in many defensive categories. Bench drove in 1,013 runs in the 1970s, more than any other player, and was named to 14 All-Star Teams. Inducted in 1989.

MAJOR LEAGUE TOTALS			
BA	H	HR	RBI
.267	2,048	389	1,376

ROD CAREW

In 1977, Rodney Cline Carew made a valiant run at the .400 mark last topped by Ted Williams in 1941, though Rod fell just short at .388. He topped the .300 plateau 15 times and the .330 mark 10 times, winning seven batting titles along the way. Carew posted 200-plus hits in four different seasons.

In 1967, Carew won the Rookie of the Year Award. He established his bat wizardry early, winning a batting title in 1969. Carew won four straight AL batting titles from 1972 to 1975. As a second baseman, the slightly built Carew took a pounding, so Twins manager Gene Mauch moved Rod to first base to extend his career. In 1977, he responded with his serious run at .400, hitting .388 with a league-leading 16 triples, 239 hits, and 128 runs. It was his sixth batting title and the largest bat title margin in baseball history. Carew was a runaway choice for the league's Most Valuable Player.

A master bunter, when he won the batting title in 1972, Carew had numerous bunt hits but not a single homer. In 1969, he stole home seven times, tying Pete Reiser's record. Carew stole more than 35 bases four times. He won his final batting title with a .333 mark in 1978. Inducted in 1991.

MAJOR LEAGUE TOTALS			
BA	H	HR	RBI
.328	3,053	92	1,015

STEVE CARLTON

Steven Norman Carlton set a record with four Cy Young Awards, won 329 games over a 24-year career, and finished second to

Nolan Ryan on the all-time strikeout list with 4,136.

Carlton broke into the St. Louis starting rotation in 1965 and blossomed in 1971, posting his first 20-win season. Unable to agree on a contract, the Cards traded him to Philadelphia. Carlton immediately recorded a season for the ages—27-10 for a team that won just 59 games. By accounting for an incredible 45.8 percent of Philadelphia's wins, he set a modern record. He was the NL leader in wins, ERA (1.97), starts (41), complete games (30), innings pitched (346), and strikeouts (310).

With the Phils, Carlton worked with strength and flexibility coach Gus Hoefling to intensify his training. One drill involved working his arm down through a vat of rice. Steve Garvey, who faced Carlton for 18 years, said that Lefty's slider was almost impossible for a right-hander to hit.

Carlton won Cy Young Awards in 1972, 1977, 1980, and 1982. He appeared in seven postseasons, going 4-2 in NLCS play and 2-2 in Series play. His best October came in 1980, when he went 1-0 in the playoffs and 2-0 in the World Series, including the clincher that gave the Phillies their first-ever world championship. Inducted in 1994.

MAJOR LEAGUE TOTALS			
W	L	ERA	K
329	244	3.22	4,136

ROLLIE FINGERS

After bringing Roland Glen Fingers up from the minors in 1969, the Oakland A's shuttled him between the bullpen and the starting rotation for three years. Finally, in 1971, Oakland manager Dick

Williams decided Fingers was best suited for relief work. Fingers responded with a team-leading 17 saves that year and 21 saves in 1972. In 1973, Williams again briefly tried Fingers as a starter, but in the 11 remaining years of his career, Fingers never made another starting appearance.

The lavishly mustachioed Rollie had his career high point in the 1974 World Series against the Dodgers. With the A's shooting for their third successive world championship, Fingers won the first game of the Series with a 4⅓-inning relief stint and then came through with two saves in the final two games to land the World Series MVP trophy.

After two more seasons with the A's, Fingers, then a free agent, signed a five-year pact with the Padres. In each of his first two seasons in San Diego, he topped the senior loop in saves, with a personal high of 37 in 1978.

Fingers had his finest season in the strike-abbreviated 1981 campaign. In 47 appearances, he collected a major-league-leading 28 saves and etched a 1.04 ERA. His banner year garnered him both the MVP and the Cy Young Awards. When he retired, Fingers had compiled a major-league-record 341 saves. Inducted in 1992.

MAJOR LEAGUE TOTALS			
W	L	SV	ERA
114	118	341	2.90

EARL WEAVER

Earl Sidney Weaver was a feisty, irascible manager in the style of John McGraw. Although he despised one-run strategies, like his spiritual mentor, he specialized in finding the perfect spots for role players and getting the most from his pitchers (his hurlers won six Cy Young Awards). His run-ins with umpires are legendary. He was tossed from nearly 100 games, but only Joe McCarthy had more 100-win seasons.

A superb minor-league manager for 11 years, Weaver got his chance with Baltimore halfway through the 1968 season. The Orioles went on to win three consecutive pennants, topping the 100-win mark each time, but won only one World Series. After a slide to third in 1972, the O's took the AL East flag again in 1973 and 1974, although Oakland kept them from the World Series. They reached the postseason again in 1979 but lost that

Series, too. Weaver ranks eighth all-time in managerial winning percentage. Inducted in 1996.

MAJOR LEAGUE TOTALS		
W	L	PCT
1,480	1,060	.583

REGGIE JACKSON

Supremely confident, Reginald Martinez Jackson loved being the center of attention. He held himself to a higher standard than most and usually delivered.

Jackson blossomed as a member of the A's in 1968, hitting 29 homers with 74 RBI. While Oakland was building a dynasty, Reggie became a superstar in 1969, leading the league with 123 runs scored and a .608 slugging percentage. In 1971, Oakland won the first of five straight West Division titles. Jack-

son hit 32 homers, not including the shot off the light tower in the All-Star Game. He matched his 32-homer output in 1973, when he won the AL MVP Award. The years from 1972 to 1974 brought three straight World Series championships as the A's, united in a dislike for owner Charles Finley, brawled their way into history.

Free agency finally broke up the A's, and Jackson set out for New York, where he clashed with Yankees manager Billy Martin and owner George Steinbrenner. But in Game 6 of the 1977 World Series, Jackson hit three homers on three swings of the bat to deliver the title to the Yanks. That feat ensured his "Mr. October" designation.

After five years in New York, Jackson moved to the California Angels, helping them to first-place finishes in 1982 and 1986. Inducted in 1993.

MAJOR LEAGUE TOTALS			
BA	H	HR	RBI
.262	2,584	563	1,702

MIKE SCHMIDT

What can one say about Michael Jack Schmidt except that he might be the greatest all-around third baseman ever?

Ironically, Schmidt's first two seasons with the Phillies showed little promise. By 1974, however, both Schmidt and the Phillies were on the move. The team landed its best finish in 10 years, and Schmidt hit 36 league-leading homers and added 116 RBI. Two years later, the Phillies captured the National League East, with Schmidt leading the league in homers for the third straight year. He also collected his first Gold Glove. In 1980, Schmidt delivered career highs with 48 homers and 121 RBI, earning the MVP Award as the Phils landed the pennant.

In the World Series, Schmidt batted .381 to help the Phils win in six games. He made another World Series appearance in 1983, then led the league both in homers and RBI in 1984 and 1986. His last great year came in 1987, when he hit 35 homers with 113 RBI.

Schmidt hit 548 home runs, retiring seventh on the all-time list; captured the National League MVP Award in 1980, 1981, and 1986; was named the MVP in the 1980 World Series; and captured 10 Gold Gloves. When he left the game in 1989, he had driven in 1,595 career runs, a total that placed him among the top 25 overall and gave him more than any third baseman in major-league history. Inducted in 1995.

MAJOR LEAGUE TOTALS			
BA	H	HR	RBI
.267	2,234	548	1,595

DON SUTTON

In his 23-year career, Don Sutton won 20 games only once, captured but a single ERA title, and never led his league in strikeouts. But his amazing durability and consistency earned him Cooperstown enshrinement in 1998.

Foremost among his statistical credentials were his 324 victories, tied with Nolan Ryan for 12th most in history. He also ranks fifth in strikeouts (3,574), seventh in innings (5,282), and 10th in shutouts (58). Having spent 14 years with the Dodgers, he is still the franchise leader in those categories. Only Ryan (23) has ever recorded more than Sutton's 21 consecutive seasons with at least 100 strikeouts.

A supremely confident competitor, his repertoire included a fastball, curve, slider, screwball, and—many charged—an illegal pitch. Whether or not he actually doctored the ball, he was delighted to use the perception as a psychological weapon.

"Sutton," commentator Tim McCarver once said of the control

artist, "paints corners like Monet painted impressions."

Major League Totals			
W	L	ERA	K
324	256	3.26	3,574

1997 INDUCTEES

None of the 1997 inductees selected by the Veterans Committee fit the classic image of a superstar, but no one denied their excellence.

Throughout the 1950s, **Nellie Fox** of the White Sox was "Mr. Second Base." Fox was a 12-time All-Star—more on guts than ability. A lump of chewing tobacco indenting his cheek, the 150-pound pepperpot retired after a 19-year career as one of the greatest glove men and contact hitters ever.

Fox, the American League's 1959 MVP, reigns as the third-toughest hitter to strike out (one every 42.7 at-bats) in history. He retired with 1,619 double plays—fewer than only Bill Mazeroski among second sackers. Major League Totals: .288 BA, 2,663 hits, 35 HR, 790 RBI.

In the Negro Leagues of the 1930s, **Willie Wells** was a stunning shortstop. Nicknamed "Devil," he had an uncanny knack for positioning, a pair of the surest hands that ever graced the game, and a wonderfully accurate arm.

The feisty Wells helped lead the St. Louis Stars to three league crowns and the Chicago American Stars to two. A two-time batting champ, he once slugged 27 home runs in an 88-game season.

Like Fox and Wells, **Tommy Lasorda** was known for the fire in his belly. Briefly a wild left-hander, his fame would come as a manager. From 1976-96, Lasorda skippered the Dodgers to six divisional titles, four NL pennants, and two world championships.

Loquacious, bombastic, profane, and outrageous—but always brimming with love for his players and the game—the man who "bled Dodger blue" was one of the great motivational leaders in sports history. Major League Totals: 1,599 wins, 1,439 losses, .526 percentage.

1998 INDUCTEES

From the Negro Leagues to the front office, the four Veterans Committees inductees of 1998 left an imprint on the game.

Larry Doby, one of three players to have played in both the Negro Leagues and major-league

World Series, joined the Cleveland Indians in 1947 as the American League's first African-American. Over the next 13 seasons, he would play in seven All-Star Games. Quiet and dignified, Doby once said, "My way to react to racial prejudice was to hit the ball as far as I could." Major League Totals: .283 BA, 1,515 hits, 253 HR, 970 RBI.

"Bullet" Joe Rogan, a Negro Leaguer from 1917-46, is perhaps the greatest two-way player this side of Babe Ruth. As a hard-throwing pitcher, his known winning percentage of .721 is assumed to be the highest in Negro League history. At the plate, Rogan twice batted .400.

George Davis was one of the premier infielders of the late 19th century, forging a 20-year career of which the best were as a New York Giant. The third baseman and shortstop batted over .300 every year from 1893-1901, with a high of .355. Though not a power hitter, Davis drove in more than 100 runs three times. Major League Totals: .295 BA, 2,660 hits, 73 HR, 1,437 RBI.

Lee MacPhail, the soft-spoken master of baseball diplomacy, helped shape the game as an administrator in the 1960s, '70s, and '80s. Initially general manager of the Orioles (with whom he was Sporting News Executive of the Year in 1966) and Yankees, he later became American League president and—because of his influential role in settling the 1981 strike—head of the Major League Players Relations Committee.

APPENDIX